T0021809

OBJECTLESSONS

A book series about the hidden lives of ordinary things.

Series Editors:

Ian Bogost and Christopher Schaberg

In association with

BOOKS IN THE SERIES

Bird by Erik Anderson
Blackface by Ayanna Thompson
Blanket by Kara Thompson
Bookshelf by Lydia Pyne
Bread by Scott Cutler Shershow
Bulletproof Vest by Kenneth R. Rosen
Burger by Carol J. Adams
Cell Tower by Steven E. Jones
Cigarette Lighter by Jack Pendarvis
Coffee by Dinah Lenney
Compact Disc by Robert Barry
Doctor by Andrew Bomback
Driver's License by Meredith Castile
Drone by Adam Rothstein
Dust by Michael Marder
Earth by Jeffrey Jerome Cohen and Linda T. Elkins-Tanton
Egg by Nicole Walker
Email by Randy Malamud
Environment by Rolf Halden
Exit by Laura Waddell
Eye Chart by William Germano
Fat by Hanne Blank
Fake by Kati Stevens
Football by Mark Yakich
Gin by Shonna Milliken Humphrey
Glass by John Garrison
Glitter by Nicole Seymour
Golf Ball by Harry Brown
Hair by Scott Lowe
Hashtag by Elizabeth Losh
High Heel by Summer Brennan
Hood by Alison Kinney
Hotel by Joanna Walsh
Hyphen by Pardis Mahdavi
Jet Lag by Christopher J. Lee
Luggage by Susan Harlan
Magnet by Eva Barbarossa
Ocean by Steve Mentz
Office by Sheila Liming
Password by Martin Paul Eve
Perfume by Megan Volpert
Personal Stereo by Rebecca Tuhus-Dubrow

Phone Booth by Ariana Kelly
Pill by Robert Bennett
Political Sign by Tobias Carroll
Potato by Rebecca Earle
Questionnaire by Evan Kindley
Recipe by Lynn Z. Bloom
Refrigerator by Jonathan Rees
Remote Control by Caetlin Benson-Allott
Rust by Jean-Michel Rabaté
Shipping Container by Craig Martin
Shopping Mall by Matthew Newton
Signature by Hunter Dukes
Silence by John Biguenet
Sock by Kim Adrian
Souvenir by Rolf Potts
Snake by Erica Wright
Spacecraft by Timothy Morton
Sticker by Henry Hoke
Traffic by Paul Josephson
Tree by Matthew Battles
Trench Coat by Jane Tynan
Tumor by Anna Leahy
TV by Susan Bordo
Veil by Rafia Zakaria
Waste by Brian Thill
Whale Song by Margret Grebowicz
Air Conditioning by Hsuan L. Hsu (Forthcoming)
Alarm by Alice Bennett (Forthcoming)
Bicycle by Jonathan Maskit (Forthcoming)
Concrete Stephen Parnell (Forthcoming)
Doll Maria Teresa Hart (Forthcoming)
Fist by nelle mills (Forthcoming)
Fog by Stephen Sparks (Forthcoming)
Grave Allison C. Meier (Forthcoming)
OK by Michelle McSweeney (Forthcoming)
Pregnancy Test by Karen Weingarten (Forthcoming)
Sewer by Jessica Leigh Hester (Forthcoming)
Skateboard by Jonathan Russell Clark (Forthcoming)
Train by A. N. Devers (Forthcoming)
Wine Meg Bernhard (Forthcoming)

Trench Coat

JANE TYNAN

BLOOMSBURY ACADEMIC
NEW YORK • LONDON • OXFORD • NEW DELHI • SYDNEY

BLOOMSBURY ACADEMIC
Bloomsbury Publishing Inc
1385 Broadway, New York, NY 10018, USA
50 Bedford Square, London, WC1B 3DP, UK
29 Earlsfort Terrace, Dublin 2, Ireland

BLOOMSBURY, BLOOMSBURY ACADEMIC and the Diana logo are trademarks of
Bloomsbury Publishing Plc

First published in the United States of America 2022

Cover design by Alice Marwick

For legal purposes the Acknowledgments on p. 144 constitute an extension
of this copyright page.

Library of Congress Cataloging-in-Publication Data

Names: Tynan, Jane, 1969- author.
Title: Trench coat / Jane Tynan.
Description: New York: Bloomsbury Academic, 2022. | Series: Object lessons
| Includes bibliographical references and index. | Identifiers: LCCN 2021055609
(print) | LCCN 2021055610 (ebook) | ISBN
9781501375163 (paperback) | ISBN 9781501375187 (epub) | ISBN
9781501375156 (pdf) | ISBN 9781501375170
Subjects: LCSH: Trench coats–History.
Classification: LCC GT2079 .T96 2022 (print) | LCC GT2079 (ebook) | DDC
391.4/609–dc23/eng/20211216
LC record available at https://lccn.loc.gov/2021055609
LC ebook record available at https://lccn.loc.gov/2021055610

ISBN: PB: 978-1-5013-7516-3
ePDF: 978-1-5013-7515-6
eBook: 978-1-5013-7518-7

Series: Object Lessons

Typeset by Deanta Global Publishing Services, Chennai, India
Printed and bound in the United States of America

To find out more about our authors and books visit www.bloomsbury.com and sign
up for our newsletters.

For Matt

I made my song a coat.
Covered with embroideries
Out of old mythologies
From heel to throat;

— *A COAT* (1914) BY WILLIAM BUTLER YEATS

CONTENTS

List of Figures xiii

Introduction 1

1 Substance 7

2 War 21

3 Mobility 35

4 Insurgency 53

5 Reportage 69

6 Heroes or Villains 85

7 Outsiders 103

8 Style 119

Conclusion 137

Postscript 143

Acknowledgments 144

Notes 145

Index 161

FIGURES

1   Marian Marsh, 1932 5

2   La Pianiste FR/AUT 2001 Isabelle Huppert, 2001 12

3   Advert for Aquascutum waterproof military coats 1916.
     Proof against rain and cold wind military trench coat,
     lined with wool, detachable fleece, fur or leather 23

4   Dampierre, July 1916 (oil on canvas). Artist: François
     Flameng (1856–1923) 29

5   V.A.D. about to set out 44

6   Flying nurses of the Ninth troop carrier command of
     United States Army Air Force at a marching drill at their
     base in England during the Second World War March
     1944 51

7   Dublin 1922. Anti-Treaty members of the Irish
     Republican Army (IRA) in Grafton Street, Dublin during
     the Irish Civil War 62

8   Left to right: Roman Karmen, Ernest Hemingway and
     camera operator Ioris Iveno. Spain, 18 September
     1937. SPUTNIK / Alamy 76

9   American actor Humphrey Bogart (1899–1957) in the
     1940s 92

10 Kay Francis, American actress, 1934–35. Taken from Meet the Film Stars, by Seton Margrave. (London, 1934–35) 94

11 THE CHEAP DETECTIVE, 1978 Peter Falk 100

12 Eine Auswaertige Affaere, Foreign Affair, A, Eine Auswaertige Affaere, A Foreign Affair with Marlene Dietrich, Jean Arthur. 1948 105

13 DRAGNET, Jack Webb, (1966) (1967–70) 106

14 Harrison Ford in a scene from film Bladerunner 1982 110

15 SHAFT, Richard Roundtree, 1971, walking past the Apollo Theatre, New York 120

16 The Trench Coat As Seen By Hardy Amies Around The 1960'S. UNITED KINGDOM. In A Street Of London, Five Trench Coats Of Different Colors Being Presented By The Friends Of Hardy Amies 123

17 BREAKFAST AT TIFFANY'S, Audrey Helburn and George Peppard, 1961 128

18 Poster advertising Burberry fashion house with Cara Delevingne in paper magazine from 2014 131

19 PRINCESS AURORA (aka ORORA GONGJU), Eom Jeong-hwa, 2005 133

20 FILM THE MATRIX BY ANDY AND LARRY WACHOWSKI. Keanu Reeves in the 1999 movie The Matrix 134

21 2006 MTV Video Music Awards Show. Beyoncé performing 'Ring the Alarm' at Radio City Music Hall in New York City, New York, United States 136

INTRODUCTION

I am not surprised when people ask why I am writing a book about the trench coat. After all, coats come in many shapes and sizes. What is so special about this one? Others get it instantly and proceed to tell their own trench coat story. My obsession with the trench coat began at least ten years ago. I might have been in the Imperial War Museum doing some research on military uniform, when it struck me that the trench coat was likely to be the only piece of kit that truly survived the First World War. From a twenty-first century perspective, trench coats show no sign of disappearing; flick through a style magazine or search social media and you will find the trench coat popping up, again and again. What is it about this seemingly unremarkable item of clothing that attracts attention? Underneath a deceptively banal exterior hides any number of fables, ghosts, myths, and hidden powers. One of the First World War's surviving artefacts, the trench coat is a material remnant of a great rupture but also a projection into a violent and alienating future.

What other cultural artefact from the past century could bring together Siegfried Sassoon, Greta Garbo, Simone de

Beauvoir, Ernest Hemingway, Philip Marlowe, and Beyoncé? What powers do trench coats bestow? Fusing textiles and substances in alchemical processes, the trench coat made fabric impregnable to water. We cannot underestimate what this flexible waterproof fabric meant to people's sense of being modern. It materialized an everyday soft strength that promised to overcome limits, ushering in a new world that invited bodies to inhabit scientific realms.

Trench coats capture the modern malaise, but they also defy the natural laws of porous fabrics and bodies. Garments might be human inventions, but they are far more pliable, fluid, and available to illusion than the 'hard' designs furnishing our homes. Clothes furnish our bodies— they bring us into being—but without a narrative fastening them to the ebb and flow of lifeways, they vanish and fade. Fashion has given this churn of styles a logical scheme (of sorts), locking garments into an ongoing cycle of recreation and reinvention. But clothes have another curious quality, in that each item only truly comes to life on the human body. Imagine isolating a garment from its hinterland; all that is left is a ghostly thing, a pile of fabric on the floor, a mess of matter in search of a pattern. As the cover of this book illustrates, a disembodied trench coat is lost, unmoored, adrift when divested of the power to inhabit a person's life. A spectral presence and remnant of its embodied form, the trench coat withers without a body or scenario to latch onto. Like botanical sketches that uproot plants from the soil—to fix their image in a frame—a coat without a body is estranged from itself, from the flow of things. In this book we are drawn outwards, from the garment itself, to the people and places the trench coat has touched, as well as the images, smells and sounds that periodically usher it into our consciousness.

At once playful, but also deadly serious, sinister yet covetable, both mundane and extraordinary, trench coats are a seemingly permanent presence. Given the endless circulation of references in fashion media, literature, TV, comics, on stage and screen, can the trench coat really surprise us? I embark on this book hoping to do just that. Organized into eight chapters, each offering a thematic episode, this book is a playful meditation on the life and times of the trench coat. Histories are braided together in episodic fashion to highlight its multiple uses and misuses. We witness the trench coat furnishing cultural narratives of the modern, and while I focus on key ruptures that saw the trench coat come into its own, there is so much more to discover.

Having been a trench coat observer for a while now, I am alive to its fictions and contradictions. One thing is certain, though, trench coats are about being out of doors, and like umbrellas, are worth taking along when venturing out. Whenever faced with the dilemma of what to wear I often end of up grabbing my trench coat; it's old, battered, and drab, but inexplicably stylish. It covers a multitude of sins. I often wonder—since they improve with age—what it takes to convince people to purchase a new one. The flood of advertisements and media images I encountered during my research suggest that the appeal might be in the detail. Blogs, media articles and advertisements for trench coats tend to obsess about their wonderfully practical details, giving the impression that a stunning truth might at last be revealed by running over the fascinating external features just one more time. When scrutinizing objects, the way people talk about them can be very revealing; with trench coats, it seems, there is a preoccupation with the surface. It may not be naturally occurring but in many ways the surface of the trench coat emulates skin. This smooth garment inspires all kinds of reactions, as if its fabricated skin creates a disturbance in the natural order of things. Having spent countless hours pondering trench coats, I too see something unorthodox in the strangely impervious surface. I return to this throughout the book.

People have been drawn to the trench coat's imperishable veneer as protection against the dangers of exposure, but I am also interested in what lies beneath the surface. A compelling skin can never fully conceal the dark secrets trench coats hold. In literature and film, we witness fabulations of social worlds inspired by the boundary it places between the body and the many dangers lurking out there, just beyond our control. When Bob Dylan drew a sinister character in his 1965 song 'Subterranean Homesick Blues,' the man-in-trench coat image delivered just the right degree of emptiness, anonymity, and menace. At the scene of Leon Trotsky's assassination in Mexico, a trench coat was cover for the deadly weapon that finally finished him.[1] Trench coats are found in dark corners,

FIGURE 1 Marian Marsh, 1932. Courtesy Everett Collection.

bear witness to undignified endings, and invariably stand in for feelings of emptiness and desperation. Many writers, artists and philosophers settled on the trench coat when all other style options were deemed too worldly, too materialistic, or just too nice. And yet they are rarely an obvious or crass style choice. Turning up in the strangest places, we have come to think of trench coats as enigmatic, but in literature, art, and media, they have been shown to emanate deadly powers. So where does their dark and dangerous energy come from? Are they a cover for our baser instincts? Or will this sinister mantle eventually render us nonentities? Such bleak outcomes should consign the trench coat to history, but the enduring fascination tells another story. Neither bleak nor hopeful, the cryptic trench coat elicits imaginative leaps into unknown realms. It plays with time, hides vulnerability, and evokes fantasy. Under the trench coat, there is no pride or shame, no success or failure, no me or you. It is the perfect place to hide.

1 SUBSTANCE

Matter

A middle-aged woman is interrupted from an afternoon nap by her seventeen-year-old daughter. As she rises from the sofa, she becomes aware of the girl's tutor standing just outside the drawing room. Resentful of this imposter's regular presence, the woman of the house exits the room to see something fierce and threatening in the body of the tutor in an ugly green mackintosh. Feeling Doris Kilman's silent scorn, Clarissa Dalloway has the sense that she is being cruelly judged for living a spoilt and indulgent life of wealth and comfort. Meanwhile, this taciturn, religious, woman gets closer to her beloved daughter, Elizabeth. Were it not for Miss Kilman, Clarissa might be free of the embattled, ugly existence of others such as her, perspiring in their cheap coats, worn down by poverty, exhibiting bitter frugality and righteousness. In Virginia Woolf's *Mrs Dalloway*, a novel set in 1920s London, the woman in the green mackintosh is for Clarissa, 'one of the spectres with which one battles at night'.[1] An outcast of the war and its enduring cruelties, the dour tutor is a profoundly unsettling presence for Clarissa. If beautiful domestic interiors suffocate her, then the worn-out body of Doris Kilman, in her wretched trench coat, haunts her more. In the interior life of the society hostess, matter holds a devastating truth.

We take matter for granted; objects, goods, fabrics, garb, stuff, debris, whether industrial or natural, weave a complex web of meaning. Matter includes all the non-human material we are likely to encounter in our daily lives and enters our consciousness when we craft our surroundings to make life meaningful. To say that matter can activate thought and feeling is one thing, but to suggest that it is constitutive of events is quite another. For philosopher Jane Bennett, the human and non-human are intertwined in a 'vital materiality' that endlessly reconfigures matter across time and space.[2] While we might be tempted to dismiss clothing as a mere mask, or indeed a conceit, it has extraordinary vitality and agency, all the while behaving as if it is dead matter. Given the creative force it exerts—its potential to make us—we might think of clothing as fugitive matter. Anthropologist Eduardo Viveiros de Castro observes of Amerindian cosmologies that clothing can be as active as the spiritual internal life of the person; in the right context, clothing, masks, and other coverings activate certain powers.[3] In contrast with the European insistence on polarizing appearance and essence, whereby adornment is commonly thought to hide some essential truth, he reveals its capacity to say something about the leakiness and permutability of bodies. Such is the basis for my meditation on the trench coat, an object that has found a circuitous path through various global events and popular narratives to emerge in renewed forms in the twenty-first century. By virtue of its longevity alone, the trench coat is deserving of our attention; but as Woolf's novel suggests, its capacity to transform and metamorphose—on the body and in the mind—also recalls the sheer vibrancy of matter. The trench coat is as alive as the landscape it occupies, or the people for whom it has animated whole ways of being. In multitudinous forms, the trench coat has been shown to be as active in creating configurations of power, politics and action as the people who invented it.

Investing an object, such as the trench coat, with such significance involves a leap of faith. This goes beyond suggesting that things are significant, or useful, or aesthetically pleasing. Scholarship on 'New Materialisms'—a new area of thought in the Humanities and Social Sciences— wholly reconfigures relationships between the human and non-human, to 'radically undermine[s] a discrete separation between humans and matter'.[4] New Materialisms prompts a re-evaluation of the material world and our place within it.[5] Turning on its head the belief that material objects or natural environments are ours to shape—are quantifiable and knowable—these debates raise the prospect that the humanist concerns of language, subjectivity and reason limit understanding of our environment. Embracing a non-anthropocentric realism, New Materialisms proposes that matter is neither passive nor governable, as humanist thought might have us believe. Digital developments, rapid climate change, and the rise of posthuman forms call into question the old idea that people have control over their environment, just as these developments create a complexity that cannot be explained by comprehending material worlds as inert and compliant. This journey through the history of the trench coat illustrates just how alive, complex, irrational, transforming, and vibrant even the most industrialized material objects can be.

According to Bruno Latour, 'all humans are the children of what they have worked on,' a perspective that grants technologies and things more agency than we are likely to give them credit for.[6] One of the conceits of the moderns, according to Latour, is their elevation of the inventor, the manufacturer, or more recently the designer. But once things are launched into the world, we have little understanding of what they go on to do. This book is not intended to elevate the trench coat as iconic, or a triumph of human ingenuity. Design might be the word we use to describe the practice of bringing useful things into being, but this designation presupposes a lot more foresight than humans are capable of. By singling out the trench coat I aim to explore the resonance of designed objects, to discover their life and vitality in times and places that lie just beyond their use value, or indeed their symbolic value. If the trench coat is an object (emerging from matter) then this book follows its various material transformations across time and space.

Let's start with common understandings of the trench coat; often regarded a design classic, it is perhaps one of the few garments that has been inserted into the modernist canon. So how might we situate trench coats within a taxonomy of things that make up what we think of as modern culture? For Elizabeth Wilson, dress is the 'frontier between the self and the not-self'.[7] We might just as easily exchange the word dress for trench coat. More than many garments, this coat comes to us as a skin that is fabricated (made), a surface, a frontier, a casing, a membrane. It is perhaps revealing that the trench coat was included in the 2017 exhibition *Items: Is Fashion Modern?* at The Museum of Modern Art in New York, a display of various items of clothing chosen for their significance to the history of design. Evidence, if we needed any, that the coat has made it into the 'timeless' category; once spent as a fashion item, it graduated to classic status, taking its place alongside jeans, the hoodie, the miniskirt and many more. Vernacular clothing items, things so commonplace that we rarely give them much thought, are transformed by the sedate museum space. To relocate fashion within wider debates on society, art, design, popular culture, and social memory, the curators select vernacular items of clothing that embody what it means to be modern.[8] In this setting, the trench coat is given a status above technocratic invention, something made, but also an object that has inspired new ways of being. Absent is the heroic designer, arousing the suspicion that material things have no origin, only journeys.

Ever on the move, objects emerge from matter to momentarily take shape only to morph into something else. Seen through the prism of commercial capitalism it is tempting to believe that consumer tastes drive change, but as the story of the trench coat reveals, multiple factors are at work in assembling objects: access to materials, craft, technology, politics, human desire, what the environment can and will yield. Living out a mercurial existence, the trench coat is made to last but then dissolves before our eyes only to be reconstituted in ever-more novel forms. But we must disentangle the material from the symbolic; after all, the reinforced textile that brought the trench coat into being slows its degradation considerably and, like many synthetic clothes, harms the natural environment.

FIGURE 2 La Pianiste FR/AUT 2001 Isabelle Huppert, 2001, Photo: Mary Evans/Ronald Grant/ Courtesy Everettt Collection.

Fashion screens such material realties in a play of magic and illusion as if every new incarnation is the first, inviting us to conveniently forget that even clothes need to live real, meaningful lives before they finally wear out. But trench coats play with time—collapsing temporalities and rhythms in theatrical fashion—to divert attention away from such material truths. As this exhibition lays bare, presenting clothes as iconic involves a paradox: objects that appear to be durable and perfectly at home in the world are often fragile and elusive.

Technology

The trench coat has complex beginnings. The story starts long before the First World War—to which it owes its name—with earlier experiments in waterproofing garments. Indigenous peoples of the Amazon found that a milky substance taken from rubber trees could waterproof their footwear and capes. In Europe, the Oilcloth, an early form of water-repellent clothing, also involved coating garments by bathing closely woven cotton or linen cloth in boiled linseed oil, a technique popular with sailors and fishermen in the 1700s. Europeans made various scientific expeditions to South America in the eighteenth-century Enlightenment, which brought them into contact with people who had been using rubber to waterproof various artefacts. On one such trip in 1736, French naturalist and mathematician Charles

Marie de la Condamine took samples of hevea latex back to Paris, having 'observed the Omagua peoples of the Solimões reaches of the Amazon using rubber to make bottles, shoes, hollow balls, and drinking syringes,' and proceeded to experiment 'with his samples upon his return to Paris, using them to waterproof a coat'.[9] Later in England, the process was industrialized.

A double textured fabric—rubber, softened by naphtha, captured within two layers of cloth—was patented in 1823 by Scottish chemist Charles Macintosh to create weatherproof material. Rubberized cotton garments made in this way were a huge innovation. Partnering up with Manchester cotton manufacturers, the firm trading as *Charles Macintosh & Co.* started a highly successful business making an array of goods, fueled by the cotton and rubber trades.[10] The northwest of England was the manufacturing centre for 'mackintosh' coats (the k was added to give the coats a distinctive name) for the United Kingdom but also across the globe. The first of the clothing trades to be carried out in factories, the making of weatherproof coats signaled the birth of 'ready to wear'. While European consumers were getting cheap clothes made by up-to-the minute technologies, this industry saw indigenous people suffering the pillaging of their environment.

Part of what was regarded as the success of industrial revolution and Empire, the waterproof garment business constituted trades that were heavily involved in the extraction and import of materials to England. Rubber was a significant commodity reaching Europeans through an exploitative network that extended to South America (and later Africa and Asia). The 'rubber barons'—or plantation owners—in South America employed thousands of people to extract and transport rubber to market in Europe, while colonized people suffered under brutal regimes of rubber extraction.[11] Enslaving indigenous people was intrinsic to a system that relied on a large workforce to tap rubber out of trees. Forced labour and the wiping out of indigenous economies were the price paid by people in the region. For Europeans, the mass-manufacture of these wonder garments might have meant progress, but economic growth was only possible through systematic human exploitation and ecological vandalism.

Factories in England were also sites of misery, where fire hazards were common, toxic chemicals irritated workers' lungs and streamlined production deskilled them. As John Tully explains, fires were 'a constant threat to those employed in gluing pieces of the raincoat together'.[12] By 1865 there was vulcanization, a process for hardening rubber that made it a resilient, pliable material with low water absorption. Vulcanization led to the introduction of a vast range of products for the industrial and domestic market, including rubber bands, hosing, tyres, erasers, and shoe soles. Amongst them, was Macintosh's 'Pocket Siphona,' a raincoat so light-weight that it could easily be rolled up to fit inside a pocket.[13] The pliability of this material inspired the rubberizing of all manner of consumer goods, but workers involved in cold vulcanization were often affected by carbon bisulphide poisoning, a problem highlighted on the pages of *The India Rubber Journal* in the late 1880s.[14] If proofing materials gave modern consumers a sense of safety, comfort and security, inside the factories there was no protection from harm, drudgery, or daily exposure to toxic fumes.

In the early days, large enterprise dominated the business of making rubberized fabric products, such as raincoats. Only factories could handle the various stages of production, a departure from the typical approach to garment-making at the time. Rubberized garment-making anticipated the mechanization of what had been a craft-based trade, taking on an industrial scale to accommodate the specialist techniques for making up the garments. Even the sewing machine had not managed to fully bring the clothing trade into the factory. Unlike any other branch of garment-making, the rubberized coat business was the first of the clothing trades to use factories.[15] Conventional tailoring was not set up to handle the rubbery fabric and outworkers were unable to complete tasks, such as proofing seams with rubber solution, and so, industrial waterproofing procedures saw the clothing trade bend to science. Mechanization, the use of scientific procedures and a huge dependence upon extractive imperial projects made the waterproof garment business a very modern sort of enterprise, one where people were sacrificed to profit, and technology drove decisions and outcomes.

For the consumer, the mackintosh brought with it another sense of being modern. Primarily an outer garment for leisure activities, including sport, the mackintosh invented a whole new way of living. It brought people outdoors, or at least gave them some comfort if already working outside. Since the mid-1800s the mackintosh was worn by British military personnel, but for civilians, the demand for the raincoat came with the rise of leisure as a distinct activity, which urged people to venture outdoors to enjoy healthy pastimes. What we might now call 'lifestyles' were, in the late 1800s, unheard of, but rapid changes saw the spread of outdoor leisure activities. Being out of doors brought with it the invention of new pastimes, and new types of clothing were designed to fit with these lifestyles. In nineteenth-century Britain recreation was not ordered nor compartmentalized but late in the century it began to be rationalized to fit with the needs of industrial capitalism.

Rational recreation extended the moral purpose of work to include improving pastimes, which brought with it new styles of sartorial display, regulating the rhythms of work and leisure.[16] Social theorist Max Weber viewed this division through the prism of the Protestant work ethic and economic imperatives so central to European modes of living, ideals encouraged through the dual improvement of hard work and useful play.[17] The idea of comfort was not just about physical protection, but clothes for leisure also made people feel at ease with being out of doors. Nobody wanted to feel out of place, either overdressed or underdressed. No one wanted to feel exposed. The soft strength of the new rubberized coats felt like a solution, on a material level, but also spoke to a desire for social mobility and access to new realms. By offering people new ways of living and being—to feel 'just right'—this branch of the leisure wear business owed its living to the new idea of consumer lifestyles.

If the appearance of water-repellent raincoats reflected the rise of the middle-classes, then weatherproofs flooded the market to satisfy their appetite for sturdy leisure clothes. Signalling the joy in discovering this idea of free time, and making the most of it, these leisure clothes were marketed as social aspiration wrapped up in the promise of an improved sense of being. Fabulous new lifestyles were fashioned through a miraculous material. Images of Victorian gentlemen riding, sailing, and hunting sold waterproof garments, such as the mackintosh, to those far removed from the country house. Thanks to the new technologies of vulcanized rubber, rainwear was cheap, accessible and was regarded by many as a wonder material.

Rainwear brought people out of doors and gave them new kinds of mobility. *Jordan Marsh & Co.* Dry Goods Catalog from 1897 features an image of two active independent young women wearing full detachable capes and skirts 'guaranteed rainproof' for 'walking, driving and travelling'.[18] That sense of freedom gives another advert in the US shopping catalogue for 'Ladies and Misses' Mackintoshes' an energy that goes beyond clothing, as if stylish rainproofs would bring women and girls into previously unknown sensual realms.[19] Promising women a shell to make them impervious to external pressures, this resistant material opened up new possibilities. Sensual pleasures awaited women who made the leap, who were intrepid enough to take to the outdoors without company. Waterproof wonder garments, marketed to a youthful market, also claimed to free the older consumer from the shackles of the domestic environment. For women this was a tempting prospect. A 1900 advertisement for 'Genuine Macintosh Waterproofs' depicts an affluent couple aboard a boat, snug in their Manchester-made capes announcing, 'In these enlightened days, every man, woman, and child wears or should wear a Waterproof Garment.'[20] Rainproof clothing became seductive; activating a sense of freedom, it nudged the prim and the fearful out of doors into unmapped zones.

The mass-produced mackintosh was affordable to own, which before long rendered it utilitarian, drab and destined to become a second-rate item.[21] By the end of the 1800s they were worn by dockers, servants and a variety of workers who had little choice but to be outdoors. Various advertisements anxiously proclaim their coats 'odourless'. India-rubber became synonymous with sweaty bodies and foul smells, such was the lack of ventilation reaching the recesses of the body. Some outfitters claimed that bad odours were associated with cheaper varieties, but smelly mackintoshes were widespread, which led to a churn of new techniques to reassure customers that the improved designs were comfortable and hygienic. It was clear that the mackintosh was losing its glow.

Before long, the mackintosh could not be seen as anything other than confining and clumsy, its artifice somehow made plain by the stench. Rubberized garments were otherworldly, perhaps unnatural, reflected in the sinister odour described by David Trotter, (with a formulation from Claude Lévi-Strauss) as 'the smell of decomposition; the raw inserting itself inside the cooked'.[22] The design was seemingly haunted by unnatural processes, dangerous factories and the colonial violence that brought it into being, working mysteriously through the fetid mackintosh. The smell made it repellent to the unsuspecting wearer and to anyone in their orbit. Neither did the wonder of entrepreneurial technology blind people to their clumsy appearance. On the Continent, the reputed bad dress sense of the British was confirmed by their love of the mackintosh, so easily excited were they by the odorous, ugly coverings. Seen as a peculiarly British indulgence, mackintoshes became a rich source of humour in French music-halls of the 1850s.[23] Their artifice, the smell, the sense that they were second-rate, along with the introduction of chemically treated outerwear all contributed to the decline of the mac. In a real sense, they were uncool. By the new century, rubberized clothing was consigned to the past and the era of the trench coat was about to begin.

2 WAR

The Trenches

A Captain with the American Expeditionary Forces (AEF) travels from New York to Liverpool in 1918, and upon his arrival in Folkestone he buys a trench coat. His is a journey into the unknown. Later he recounts, 'The wool lining disappeared when the French rifled our baggage in August, but the coat stayed with me through the war. I slept in it every night.'[1] From the time he arrived in Calais in April 1918 to the end of the war, the trench coat was Robert Patterson's constant companion. Raw and unprepared, American soldiers joined the war to find scenes of devastation on the western front, where they witnessed landscapes and bodies ripped apart by violence. In this hellish place, Patterson's sole reference point was the trench coat. Upon arrival, it might have been the only familiar thing he could fit into this wretched alien landscape.

It is not clear when the new chemically treated garments were first named 'trench coats' but in December 1914 *Punch* carried an advertisement for *Thresher and Glenny*'s 'Thresher

Trench Coat' at a cost of six guineas.[2] Five months into the First World War, this first mention boasts the coat's 'Wind, Wet and Mud Resisting' qualities, a steer for soldiers going to the western front. Before this, firms such as *Burberry* and *Aquascutum* were big players in the business of chemically treated showerproof garments catering for the upper end of the market. *Aquascutum* translates from Latin to mean 'water shield,' a name that nurtured the firm's reputation for making durable waterproof outerwear, underlined by vignettes from military men and explorers. *Burberry* also positioned themselves as suppliers of stylish outdoor garments with a military edge. Thomas Burberry's gaberdine was an innovation (he patented) that made waterproof twill fabric breathable by coating the individual cotton or wool yarns. 'Burberry Overcoats' showcased their special weave and proofing system, which, as one of their adverts claims, 'scientifically combine' to resist inclement weather 'without engendering unhealthy heat.'[3] Innovations such as these made the protective qualities of the cloth almost invisible.

A later advert from *Punch* illustrates *Burberry's* approach; alongside an image of an affluent man playing golf the text recommends the raincoat 'for Sportsmen and civilians— men whose duties or pleasures are out-of-doors.'[4] Rational recreation and military adventure meld in this seamless image of social aspiration. By the First World War, various firms were making the 'trench coat' across the United Kingdom, chiefly in England. An optional item of dress for officers on the western front, the coat got its name from the trenches that

AQUASCUTUM REGD.
TRENCH COAT

THE MOST RELIABLE MILITARY WATERPROOF PRODUCED.

Lined Wool. Detachable Fleece, Fur, or Leather.
Absolutely proof against Rain and Cold Winds.

From the Lieut.-Col. Commanding a Lowland Battalion in France:—

"I should like you to know that I have given one of your fleece-lined Aquascutums a very severe trial during six months' trench work out here. I have nothing but praise for its wet- and rain-resisting qualities, and it is free from several glaring faults which handicapped coats of two other makers, which I have had to wear for my sins. So far as durability is concerned, it does not look as if I would have to call upon you for a renewal for some considerable time."

The original of above letter may be seen by anyone interested.

The Coat that has given satisfaction to Officers who have been in the Trenches during the cold wet months of the year.

AQUASCUTUM, Ltd., *By appointment to His Majesty the King.*

Waterproof Coat Specialists for over 50 years.

100, Regent Street, LONDON, W.

FIGURE 3 Advert for Aquascutum waterproof military coats 1916. Proof against rain and cold wind military trench coat, lined with wool, detachable fleece, fur or leather. © Illustrated London News Ltd/Mary Evans.

ominously snaked across the countryside at war. It was not a regulation issue item and only officers were allowed to wear them. British army infantry, on the other hand, were kitted out in regulation uniforms, which included boots, braces, service cap, puttees, jacket, and greatcoat. An 'out of line' item, the greatcoat was not for the trenches and normally left with the soldier's pack behind the lines.[5] Easily weighed down by mud, cumbersome, and heavy once water-logged, the greatcoat gained a reputation for impracticality. Officers had the option of purchasing the more practical trench coat, a lighter cover to give them greater mobility in the field. In the regulations for First World War British soldiers, the greatcoat conformed to a standard pattern developed by Commandant Emile Charles Lavisse for whom the 'general shape or style of the overcoat or cloak is … a garment cut full, and which can be tightened at will to the body by means of a belt around the waist, and the skirts of which descend even to the middle of the calf of the leg'.[6] This same military shape styled the trench coat.

Coats themselves went further back. Starting with the introduction of tailoring, a sculpting practice to reveal the contours of the body, the etymology of coat suggests it derives from the word for a mantle or robe. From the Old French *cote*, it referred to a 'coat, robe, tunic, overgarment'.[7] Trench coats have the 'frock,' derived from the frock coat worn by eighteenth-century gentlemen. Then, it was a sartorial code of social politeness, but the frock feature was discarded with the introduction of looser modern styles, as the overcoat spread to a wider range of social groups. Relaxed silhouettes were somewhat reversed with the appearance of trench coats, however, which brought back the fitted waist in the early twentieth century. Body contours had been a sign of masculine power and privilege, but returned with this repurposed image of the self-contained, moral man. The trench coat might have been a fresh new design when it first appeared at the start of the twentieth century, but its close-fitting waist combined with a loose style represented a nostalgic return to older ideas of manliness. Emphasizing the shoulders and waist reinstated traditional power markers, while the rest of the body went undercover. Both hard and soft, a cloak and a tailored garment, exclusive but cheap, the trench coat emerged as a hybrid mix of styles and attitudes.

Given the sheer volume of officers recruited to the British army, war was good for business as far as trench coat makers were concerned. Alongside the many consumer goods renamed or repurposed to intensify their link with the war, the trench coat's military edge appealed to patriotic civilians at home. Army officers who fought with British regiments could purchase their trench coat from the same retail outlets as their civilian counterparts. In contrast to the pre-war make-up of the army, the initial recruitment drive filled regiments with civilians in uniform. Trench coats were sold by retailers such as *Gamages,* a London store specializing in military paraphernalia, and in 1915 *The Tatler* carried one of their adverts with gift suggestions for 'Britain's "Blue" and "Khaki" Boys,' featuring the service trench coat.[8] Presented as a commonplace consumer item, the trench coat could be acquired easily and cheaply by civilians far from the trenches of France and Belgium. As War Office dress regulations show, the trench coat was an optional item of kit for officers; the only rain-resistant outer garment listed is the 'Waterproof Cape'.[9] Neither a regulation garment, nor an item of kit worn by the rank and file, the trench coat had an in-between kind of status. An American soldier in transit, such as Patterson, could easily purchase the coat in an English coastal town before his dispatch to France. For him the urgency of the conflict was real, but the availability of trench coats made the fantasy readily available to all; civilians could casually purchase their own bit of military action from the local department store.

Kenneth Durward of London's West End also competed in the crowded raincoat business, and sold their own 'Durward Trench Coat,' as did *Zambrene*, who promoted their wares with finely executed lithographic prints—one held in the Imperial War Museum poster collection—featuring images of handsome army officers in windswept landscapes.[10] A wartime *Aquascutum* advertisement quotes a letter, apparently written in 1916, from a Lieutenant Colonel commanding a battalion in France: 'I have given one of your fleece-lined Aquascutums a very severe trial during six months trench work out here. I have nothing but praise for its wet-and rain-resisting qualities.'[11] A drawing of an officer wearing the classic trench coat style reveals a belt, flaps to shield wind, shoulder epaulettes, and sleeve loops to keep the body warm. Images of military elitism did no harm to domestic sales of the trench coat.

Various models of the coat emerged in wartime. Some had large pockets to keep maps dry, while cleverly placed flaps and vents prevented the common problem of trapped sweat. A good proofing system and a range of external details engineered a design that was light, convenient, and comfortable. The 'Tielocken' featured many of the details that went on to form the classic trench coat style, but unlike the *Aquascutum* version it had no buttons making it easier to adjust for changing weather conditions. A double-breasted coat with an innovative fastening system, the characteristic shoulder epaulettes and belted waist gave it a distinctive trench coat quality. Encasing the body for warmth in cold winds but light and cool on warmer days, this must have felt like a futuristic covering. During wartime, this invention was a boost to morale. It shielded embattled bodies and evoked fantasies of wonderous technologies overcoming the dangers for soldiers at the front. *Burberry* emblazoned the words 'Security – Comfort – Distinction' across the top of the 'Tielocken' advert, a trick that many firms used to give the impression that factory-made items could retain a distinctive tailor-made quality. With the trench coat, everything had changed and yet, miraculously, nothing had been disturbed.

Camouflage and Pollution

Consumers were given something new with the trench coat, and a certain excitement surrounded the distinctive clothing technologies that brought it into being. But technologies of war also found uniform design undergo various changes in the early century; clothing became critical to survival on the modern industrialized battlefield. Functional camouflage was essential for First World War soldiers faced with new military technologies that made conspicuous features a matter of life and death. Given the tactical advantage camouflage gave those in the field of battle, the British army (and various other armies) took to developing designs that made soldiers less conspicuous. As aerial reconnaissance and smokeless guns placed fighting soldiers in mortal danger, the army quickly realized that distinctive items were making them a target in the field. The conspicuous styles of the officer corps meant danger, which caused them to distrust riding-boots, leather puttees and what Paul Fussell described as 'melodramatically cut riding breeches'.[12] Splashy designs made officers all too visible. A retreat from battlefield spectacle saw the rise of the practical, functional, drab-coloured trench coat, alongside various functional styles to protect combatants. Before long, the cumbersome greatcoat was largely replaced by the light, water-repellent coat.

Trench coats arrived on the threshold of the modern world alongside new forms of warfare, lending this techno-garment a certain mystique in the eyes of civilians. When uniform-making went out to the civilian trades, the limited capacity of army clothing factories to meet the demands of the war effort, found outfitters supplying mass-produced garments to officers. Coinciding with the rise of 'new tailoring,' the raincoat business could market itself as simultaneously made-to-measure *and* mass-produced. Consumers were invited to believe that they could acquire good quality mass-produced clothes at significantly less cost than, say, a Savile Row suit. Images of elite military types in rolling landscapes completed the fantasy, fusing 'tailored' garments with scientifically made shells to signify this new modernity. Material goods might have invested soldiers' bodies with the mythical power of science and technology, but the reality of shrapnel, tanks and toxic gases were doing their dirty work in the battlefields of the western front.

FIGURE 4 Dampierre, July 1916 (oil on canvas). Artist: François Flameng (1856–1923) Credit: Musee de l'Armee, Paris. Courtesy Bridgeman Images.

Writers commonly chose the trenches of the First World War to describe the loss of innocence many experienced in the conflict. Summing up the defensive position soldiers took, and the dangers they faced, the trenches were amateur, ramshackle, dirty, damp, smelly and thoroughly squalid. In his *Memoirs of a Fox-Hunting Man,* Siegfried Sassoon, in the guise of George Sherston, describes a pathetic scene in the trenches. Upon entering the dug-out he finds his amiable company commander Captain Barton 'sitting on a box at the rough table, with a tin mug and a half-empty whisky bottle. His shoulders were hunched and the collar of his trench-coat was turned up to his ears.'[13] The textures of the trenches are brought to life in this 'morose cramped little scene,' where the drab trench coat resonates with the dank and musty air, razor wire and sandbags, chalk lumps falling from the ceiling and flickering yellow candlelight.[14] For Paul Fussell, the war 'domesticates the fantastic and normalizes the unspeakable,' reflected in trench formations that sum up the endless replication and sinister uniformity of these bleak hide-outs.[15] Military technology found new ways to blow bodies apart, seen hanging from trees in no man's land because nobody would dare to retrieve them. Mass slaughter turned the mud red. A conflict with such grotesque material transformations approximate what Mary Douglas described as 'matter out of place.'[16] Her insights into what constitutes pollution lie at the heart of the paradox of a surface (the impervious reinforced fabric of the trench coat) designed to seal bodies off from danger (boasting all kinds of protective qualities) but turns out to be no protection at all; once tested in the field, the soldier's body is promptly violated. Myths of bodies made impervious to risk were shattered in the fields of France and Belgium. Matter was significant to understanding what took place in the field of battle, events that brought the trench coat into the sinister realm of violence and suffering. An imperishable coat it may have been, but was it was no defence against death and wounding in the trenches. The modern world might have its wonders, but it was also hellish. Bodies become fleshy matter and the western front a scorched earth, enough to demolish any illusions of a future built on order and security.

Trench coats were a peculiar kind of consolation in the face of mass slaughter. Dystopian visions of the trenches on the western front were only available later, but for wartime civilians trench coats held out the hope of improved performance on land and sea. It might be worth asking why they chose to name a glamorous coat after such a dystopian landscape. But the home front was replete with fantasies of military heroism, including images of durable trench-coated military men, and as time went on were a thin veil over what was starting to look like a catastrophe. A defence against anxiety, images transformed a complex and painful reality into a more palatable version of the conflict, fought by military heroes in rolling landscapes bravely facing a knowable enemy. People had become accustomed to seeing military uniform as something remote from daily life, a distant and spectacular sign of fashionable adventuring. In this war, military experience was demystified, in part due to the visual and material transformations that domesticated military styles, bringing drab khaki and equally drab trench coats closer to those on the home front. But the trench coat was not just a wartime image; the coat was matter, travelling as it did from home to battlefront, and sometimes back again. Returning soldiers, for instance, were likely to witness trench coats coming home. It would have been unremarkable for a returning veteran to see his bank manager in a trench coat, resembling the one worn by his army Captain at the front. If he had been one of the 'temporary gentlemen' recruited for the duration of the war, then he would have owned one himself. If he was lucky, the coat came home with him, intact.

Beneath the triumphant and manly physique presented in posters and advertisements lurks a sinister narrative of bodies institutionalized by the army. A uniform designed to get a grip on minds and bodies was an unlikely draw for consumers, yet trench coats could mean so many different things: a meme and a material object, a souvenir and a sign of unity, a stand-in for unspeakable suffering, but also a reminder of the drift to normalizing violence. Out of the catastrophe of war came the trench coat, an object as vibrant and alive—and as dark and unforgiving—as the landscape it inhabited. Wartime discourse was all about ushering bodies to the front line. Various institutions, both private and public, circulated the image of the outdoor man in a trench coat—a civilian in uniform—throughout British popular culture. By fusing outdoor fun and war, by domesticating danger and creating fantasies of martial adventure abroad, the trench coat idea marked the militarizing of the home front. In fashionable form, the man-in-trench-coat image was alluring, acting as recruiting agent and propaganda image. Even when the full horrors of the trenches became known, the name endured, a chilling reminder of just how domesticated the militarizing narrative had become.

In many ways, the trench coat story was a predictor of the approach of mass consumer fashion, with its synthetic fibres and factory-made clothes. Its entanglement with the politics of the First World War found the trench coat the site of multiple meanings: it normalized violence, boosted industrial productivity, and afforded social mobility. Above all, trench coats generated huge profits due to the ease of their mass-production and the access British firms had, first to the natural resource of rubber, and then to chemical industrial processes. Part of a larger project to style bodies for industrialized futures, the trench coat story would involve further encounters between utility and fashion.

3 MOBILITY

Leisure and Work

Dandies, bespectacled Cambridge fellows, busy lawyers, Bishop's wives, Old Generals, and a variety of pet dogs. This is what writer George Augustus Sala claimed to have seen on the cliffs of Capri in the late 1880s. But amongst the various English tourists on the cliffs, he was struck by the elite visitors, including 'her majesty's ministers in plaid shooting jackets' and 'archdeacons in waterproof coats'.[1] Such was the reputation of English elites for pragmatic dressing that they were easy to spot, and ready for caricature. In Continental newspapers they were personified 'by an aristocrat with a monocle, a sinister capitalist in a top-hat, or a spinster in a Burberry' according to George Orwell.[2] He disputed the notion that the England of the property-owning classes could stand in for the national character, but was ready to admit that the population largely tended towards 'exaggerated class distinctions, and an obsession with sport'.[3] Clothes were powerful markers of social class in England and the sartorial style of the upper classes centred around their sporting pastimes. Patterns of leisure had by the 1940s—when Orwell wrote his book *The English People*—extended sports clothing to a wider range of social groups, but the dominant image of gentility still held a certain allure. The conspicuous privilege of the land-owning aristocratic classes gave their leisure habits, and in turn their clothes, a romance that continues to make the trench coat desirable. Despite its chief mission to equip the wartime officer corps, auxiliaries and many more besides, the trench coat retains this sense of elitism, as if it can eschew social class tensions, while remaining entrenched in them, a paradox I explore later with the various marketing techniques that recast the coat as a 'heritage' fashion item.

The trench coat attached to images of Anglo-Saxon nobility, helped along by wartime advertising images of elite military types in lush landscapes having the time of their life. When Nancy Mitford's book *Noblesse Oblige* comes along in 1956, it indulges many of the English stereotypes so despised by Orwell, with amusing but snobbish vignettes mapping the characteristics of the English aristocracy. One essayist in the book, Alan S. C. Ross (who catalogued linguistic class indicators) concludes that by the 1950s '*Burberry* and *Raincoat*' are 'rather old-fashioned U' (upper-class), a designation prevalent before 1914, when the upper classes preferred an 'expensive kind of Macintosh'.[4] Amongst the many witty diversions in *Noblesse Oblige*, this one is revealing; by associating the trench coat with pre-war upper-class lifestyles the writer confirms the exclusive status of the garment in the popular psyche by the mid-century, leaving behind the image of the frugal and impoverished ghosts of the war.

At a time when British stately homes and aristocratic manners were dissolving, Mitford's book captures the sense of melancholy many felt for a vanishing world, while betraying a hidden desire to revive it in the face of a rising middle class. For the writers, the trench coat (they call it macintosh) represents an antiquated world of aristocratic privilege, untainted by social changes brought about by war. Elsewhere, trench coats were regarded as 'practical, utilitarian garments that were mainly aligned with de-individuating activities such as army or household services'.[5] Trench coats were hardly a symbol for those acting decisively in the world, but a uniform for workers and civilians enlisted to a catastrophic life-changing war. Yet in the minds of Mitford and her essayists, the 'Burberry' retained its association with elite lifestyles. Mass-produced and widely available, trench coats were neither exclusive nor posh but durable workwear for a range of occupations, worn by soldiers, servants, and factory workers. Once the war had been consigned to history, the trench coat could be repurposed to signify military strength and the return of middle- and upper-class dominance. Mythical images of trench-coated Englishmen supplanted the reality that they had clothed the workers for the war effort and embodied that transforming experience.

Women started wearing trench coats in their numbers in military service and other wartime work in the 1910s.

Registration for war work saw working-class and middle-class women entering industry, agriculture, commerce, and the civil service. But after 1916, the engineering and chemical trades attracted women dissatisfied with the poor wages and relative lack of freedom in domestic service and garment-making jobs. Trench coats, for example, could be seen on women working at the Woolwich Arsenal in London, a factory making armaments and ammunition for the British Armed Forces during the First World War. This dangerous and precise work demanded the right gear, given the dangers of military hardware manufacture. Women workers operated machinery, assembled detonators, filled bullets, and made shell cases.[6] Considering the risk of explosion at the munitions factories, a strict uniform policy required workers to wear anti-spark wooden clogs, protective clothing, and prohibited them from having jewellery or hairpins.[7] One portrait of seven anonymous women in belted coats reflects the policy of protective clothing inside the Royal Munitions Factory in London.[8] Such a photograph was likely staged to publicize the hoped-for wartime contribution of female civilians. It also captures the optimism of that moment, illustrating the ready assimilation of civilians into the war effort. Kitted out in military-style coats, uniformity heightens their militarized appearance; but individuality seeps through, as if this glimpse into the lives of these seven London women discloses some truth about the pressure placed on wartime civilians to conform. In belted buttoned-up double-breasted coats, the regimented look embeds the women in the complex of industrialized warfare.

The militarizing of femininity aligned with the political cause of suffragettes, for whom the war held out hope that women would be visible in roles normally associated with men. For young munitions workers at the Royal Arsenal Woolwich the long proofed belted coat with large practical pockets obscures their civilian clothes underneath.[9] Erasure of fleshiness, vulnerability and individuality was the psychic work of uniforming workers. For wartime women, uniforms reimagined fleshy bodies through fantasies of rationality, recasting them in the image of the machines they operated. Even at a distance from front-line action, military-style uniform was attempting to impose disciplinary techniques on civilian bodies. Amongst the range of uniforms worn by women in wartime, the trench coat—with its impermeable surface—shielded them from machines and toxic chemicals, but perhaps also offered sanctuary from the demands of conventional femininity.

Automobility for Nurses

Militarizing women so visibly was not met with widespread support, given its counter-current to the prevailing 'cult of domesticity'. Aligning women auxiliaries with male soldiers attracted attention, and at times hostility; after all, they were taking on roles normally reserved for men. One such organization was a medical aid unit, the Voluntary Aid Detachment (known as VADs), set up to provide care for military personnel in field hospitals and convalescent hospitals nearer home. Serving on the Western Front, in Mesopotamia and Gallipoli, the largely untrained VADs were enlisted from middle-class, well educated, younger sections of the female population in the United Kingdom, though members also came from Canada. In various photographs British VADs wear long, waxed cotton trench coats over their uniforms. The First Aid Nursing Yeomanry (FANY) were another unit recruited to act as critical first aiders on the Western Front. A photograph from the Imperial War Museum depicts these first female ambulance drivers in France in 1914—a unit attached to the Belgian army—with female service personnel shown in the long-weatherproofed coats.[10] Advertisements for trench coats were everywhere. Junior Stores of Regent Street sold trench coats to 'Women on Active Service attached to Military Forces,' including 'Ladies' Khaki Trench Coats' impervious to rain and wind yet, 'more "dressy" than any previously designed Trench Coat for Ladies'.[11] Conforming to the usual trench coat design, this model has an added 'storm flap,' a protective feature designed to prevent water from entering the coat as it runs down the shoulders. Here, a navy-blue triple proofed twill trench coat—given the military name 'The Patrol,' for nurses on active service—reveals the militarizing narrative at work.[12]

Early in the war, uniforms on women attracted negative attention, ranging from opinions in print to verbal abuse directed at FANYs in khaki, castigating them for trespassing on masculine territory.[13] But some were fascinated by uniformed women. In 1916, Canadian VADs drivers caught the attention of journalist and novelist F. Tennyson Jesse, who was clearly impressed by their androgynous appearance, especially their 'goggles and gauntlets and the dashing black leather trench coats and aviator helmets'.[14] Newfoundland women VAD recruits doubtless enjoyed the new sense of freedom they gained from driving around in functional, comfortable clothing. Social mobility for wartime women was bound up with automobility, given the prominence of female drivers in the war. Women's automobility had attracted the attention of coat and cloak makers long before the war, when they produced motoring coats made of leather or rubber, often worn with waterproof hoods and goggles. Mobility, in every sense, gave impetus to a rise in demand for trench coats and the various models of water-repellent outerwear. Ambulance drivers, though, attracted a different kind of attention and their uniform was singled out to undermine their claim to mobility.

Independence for women was bound up with questions of visibility, how to be out of doors, and what style of encounter they might have venturing beyond the security of the home. Travelling, walking, driving, and playing sport could be embodied by practical, weatherproof clothing. As new modes of being were reimagined through various types of clothes and accessories, images of a modernized femininity drew from military attitudes and styles. There was a curious obsession with the uniforms worn by women drivers, not least because this visible sign of their mobility—or their automobility—posed a threat to business as usual. Coats for the US Red Cross Motor Corp bore a striking resemblance to the classic war trench coat, with its belted waist and wide lapels. Masculine flaps and epaulettes were avoided. The Library of Congress holds a 1917 photograph of an early recruit—in a trench coat, complete with armband and service cap—proudly standing on the footplate of her car.[15] Florence J. Borden Harriman headed up the first group, a wealthy socialite and suffragette for whom the corps was an opportunity to make a bid for women's social mobility. It attracted similarly affluent women who were more likely to own and drive a car. In common with other photographs publicizing the work of the corps, this image highlights style and attitude, as if recruits and their publicists were aware that the camera would make history; they responded by flaunting an air of bold confidence. A uniform—consisting of a long grey coat, high lace up boots, leather belt and service cap with the American Red Cross insignia—confirmed their audacity, and quickly made them a focus of public interest. Harriman's daughter Ethel designed the uniform and as the older woman recalled, 'Some said their husbands would never, never let them wear such things … Once we got the coats and breeches made, they became so popular that the national motor service of the Red Cross followed the example of our Washington Corps.'[16] Public disputes over the breeches fussed about their manly qualities, revealing anxieties that durable, modern clothes might give women ideas, a too-visible sign of their mobile, active roles in the war effort. Manly coats were not the problem, as such, but they were symptomatic of a larger threat, namely that militarized women might blur gender boundaries.

A striking photograph of suffragette Armine Gosling wearing an 'ankle length leather trench-coat, gloves, and aviator cap' confirms the alliance between wartime work and feminism.[17] Though many of the subjects are unknown, one photograph taken on the Western Front around 1918, held in The National Library of Scotland, reflects new styles of being the war afforded women, evident in the image of a Canadian VAD driver in black shiny trench coat and goggles.[18] Taken by Ernest Brooks, the first British official war photographer assigned to the Western Front, his photographs spread the word that (even) women were being recruited to military discipline. As the images suggest many were far from reluctant. Circulating in the media—and often a source of fascination—images and stories gave the impression that uniformed women were strange and unnatural. Recruits, however, often visited commercial studios to pose in khaki, basking in their newly acquired military status. Images of VADs reflected the severity of the wartime crisis, citing gender reversal as irrefutable evidence that the upheaval was felt in every household. After all, if women were wearing manly uniforms, then there must be something to be worried about.

FIGURE 5 V.A.D. about to set out. Photograph by Ernest Brooks from First World War 'Official Photographs'. Reproduced by kind permission of the National Library of Scotland.

A dark waterproof coat could speak the unspeakable, suggesting dangerous adventures, mud and blood, death and injury. The underlying message was that citizens should be grateful for such sacrifices, encapsulated by the sight of women surrendering their femininity. Never mind the reality that women might have been relieved to slip into roles where they could do substantial work and forego the indignity of being decorative appendages to men. Masculine decorations— here trench coats and goggles—might have given women opportunities to explore gender fluidity. The cross-dressing woman constituted a double threat, as Juliette Pattinson observes: 'she undermined the masculinity of the male soldier and negated her own femininity'.[19] If the sight of uniformed women performing manly masquerade heightened gender anxiety, then it was compounded by the cloaking effects of trench coats, which kept onlookers guessing as to what lay underneath.

Bringing the War Home

Militarized women threatened to disturb Edwardian gender relations, but their image made a bold claim to the national story by visibly shouldering military burdens. Many suffragists supported this symbolic bid for equality, including campaigner Emmeline Pankhurst, who called for obligatory national war service in Britain.[20] The war was an opportunity for suffragettes to demonstrate women's capacity for full citizenship, a stance that transformed their status from troublemakers to patriots. Both symbols of patriotic service and a threat to male hegemony, uniformed women perplexed onlookers. If service uniforms made women conspicuous then great care was taken to render them unequal to their male counterparts. Women received less pay and held civilian status; discrimination even extended to the redesign of more 'feminine' insignia. Just as social class, race and nationality were marked by uniform codes in the military, gender was also carefully policed during wartime, to preserve white, male entitlement to military status in an institution that counted on the political reliability of its members. The Women's Army Auxiliary Corps were, for example, forbidden by Britain's War Office from saluting or being saluted, a paradigmatic military gesture of mutual respect seemingly protected for men.[21]

The problem for those making the rules was the calamitous scale of the conflict itself, which made it impossible to stem the flow of women into the military, such was the demand for service personnel. It was no longer practical to confine women to their usual roles as nurses, cooks, and clerks; increasingly they were called upon to do the muscular work of driving and digging. To ameliorate the threat that mobilizing women posed, visible markers such as uniform managed them downwards, in a society rattled by the spectre of gender upheaval. If only women could get on with the job and stop getting ideas! Internal dialogue must have been troubled by the problems that recruiting women posed, but the calculus was that the war's end would see women return to the normality of domesticity, and invisibility. To allay public anxieties caused by gender transgression they made appeals in the media. One such article in the London *Times* did not interpret public visibility as a sign of trespass but rather a show of earnestness. Recruits were shown to reflect the new patriotic spirit of public service that would mark the end of fashionable leisure.[22] A restoration of essential British values was the subtext, an optimistic but flawed version of events to give the impression that clothes, and the new styles of being they ushered in, were nothing to fear. Women in trench coats were not the renegades they appeared to be, or so the story went. Branches of the media were content to interpret the sight of uniformed women as a welcome return of a traditional spirit of patriotism. Seeking to present women in khaki as a patriotic stopgap solution for war work took attention away from the widely held suspicion that they were pitching for men's jobs.

The Tatler in 1917 featured an advert for *Barkers* 'Reliable Trench Coat' sold in the Women's Service Section of the department store on Kensington High Street in London.[23] A place where nurses and war workers purchased 'every detail of their uniform or equipment', the Services Section sold a trench coat made with proofed cotton, a 'life saver in bad weather'.[24] Featuring the belted waist, wide lapels, and sleeve loops, this style has no shoulder epaulettes, cutting what was thought to be a more feminine silhouette. As the war progressed, trench coats were increasingly conspicuous in consumerist and patriotic discourses, and like the servicewomen who wore them, were thought to be reliable. Late in the war the *New York Times* carried an advert calling on suppliers to increase their stocks, announcing that the 'various types of "trench coats" for women are in exceptionally good demand'.[25] Trench coats for women were no longer an oddity. Women's magazines such as *Home Chat* juxtaposed manual labour and fashion in ways that detached fashion from leisure, fragmenting the range of available dress codes, a shift that reflected a wider pattern to renegotiate gender identities.[26] With the prevalence of trench coats for women in active service, they were less likely to be interpreted as a fashion item, and instead took on attributes of utility and action. Attempts were made, however, to collapse utility and style. In 1918, *Harper's Bazar* (as the American magazine was called then) carried a promotion for a coat with classic styling that could easily be mistaken for a regular consumer fashion item, a gift for 'the woman in service' and 'the most convincing badge of service'.[27] But by this time the war was ending.

If new wonder garments freed women from the shackles of the domestic environment by inviting them outdoors, the trench coat embodied fresh and enlightened ways of being. For women, the trench coat promised a leap into modernity. The trench coat's unisex quality with its connotations of rational leisure came to materialize new stylistic attitudes and social positions as it became entangled with the politics of the First World War. Militarizing civilian women and men was one of its incarnations, and in so doing, the trench coat became symptomatic of blurred gender boundaries. Women's experiences were not all about agency and empowerment, however, and following the war, Evadne Price—in her semi-biographical novel under the pseudonym Helen Zenna Smith—wrote about her work with VADs. Here, inconvenient realities seep through in her account of days spent cleaning engines, carrying out repairs and cleaning up vomit and blood from inside of the ambulance. Despite the drudgery of the work, and the food—'canteen filth' as she called it—the comradery kept the women going until Nell found herself holding her friend Tosh dead in her arms, 'soaking my overcoat with blood. Dead.'[28] Marking the moment in the novel when Nell loses her innocence, the blood of her friend seeps into her military coat, contaminating the potential the war held for young women like her. When she leaves war work to return home, dividing her kit between remaining pals, she decides to keep her overcoat, which was 'deeply stained where Tosh's head rested,' resolving that she must wear it.[29] Her account transforms the coat's military symbolism into a poignant touchstone of loss, signifying Nell's disenchantment, and perhaps the war weariness that had eventually crept across civil society.

Militarized appearances presented a face of uniformity and unity against a common enemy, but paradoxically for women, this involved non-conformity to familiar gendered relations. In the end, the visual complex of industrialized warfare gave rise to its own contradictions. A sign that war had come home, uniformed women stretched the military symbolism too far for the status quo to hold, disrupting the taken-for-granted stability that structured gender around public and private divisions. Trench-coated women became a common sight, and for some a private hell, but the project did modernize femininity for the war effort. Was this the spirit of the 'New Woman' waiting for an opening to emerge?

Considering the force of suffragism, a discourse of military modernity gave shape and texture to women's emancipation from the private sphere, a project that had largely been the preoccupation of activists before the war. The First World War gave the New Woman public sanction, supported by a compliant media, and enabled by branches of government and the military. Most of all, though, the idea of what constituted the New Woman materialized in uniforms, goggles, boots, trench coats and all manner of military-style clothing. As Lucy Noakes points out, women's civilian fashions during wartime reflected military styling even if wearing the actual uniform was typically regarded as a cheeky trespass on male space and authority.[30] Modern fashion was already reshaping perceptions and experiences of femininity, but the challenge uniformed women posed brought their bodies in line with the modernity of the new century. A military modernity might not have been the kind of emancipation some feminists hoped for, but many narratives of the New Woman in the period reflect on self-fashioning as an access point to change.

Leisure itself took on new meanings for women once it was made clear that public space was not available to them without a fight. But presenting as female, and what that meant, became contested as an outward symptom of inner conflicts. Fashion mapped out the boundaries of the female body, but wartime changes found it reinscribed with new meanings. Various fashionable images circulating before, during, and after the war belied the significance the trench coat had for women; how it materialized an enlarged sense of being, how it made their work visible and critical to a national story. The female bombmakers and ambulance drivers represented the recoil from conflict, reflecting the reality that not everything aligns with the carefully scripted national story. Old certainties can implode. War came home in the form of trench coats for women, not as a fashionable accessory, but evidence of their work in risky occupations, and their claim on a uniform designed for daring acts. Co-opted by women in the war for liberation, the seemingly banal coat took on a whole new set of meanings. As trench coats spread, they became part of the toolkit for emancipation and survival.

FIGURE 6 Flying nurses of the Ninth troop carrier command of United States Army Air Force at a marching drill at their base in England during the Second World War March 1944 (Photo by Mirrorpix / Mirrorpix via Getty Images).

4 INSURGENCY

Anarchic Disorder

A young woman in a beret and trench coat fires a gun at a Paris Photographic rifle range in Porte d'Orléans, Paris. Her male companion watches, urging her on. The 1929 photograph captures a playful moment for young lovers Simone de Beauvoir and Jean-Paul Sartre. This is the year they met. Standing beside de Beauvoir in a three-piece suit, Sartre's hand rests on her shoulder; eyes shut, she clasps the gun with both hands.[1] Following the First World War, photographic shooting galleries gained popularity and for intellectuals were a source of fascination. Once she shoots her target, de Beauvoir receives the snapshot as a souvenir of her mock-violent act. From the 1920s onwards, guns and trench coats were linked in so many images and allusions in literature and film, not least because combatants had worn them in the trenches. But trench coats no longer told tales of bravery; by this time, they were a symbol of survival.

Once it had shaken off the image of patriotism and conformity, the trench coat began to imply shadowy existences, insurgent behaviour, and intellectual complexity. Jeff Shantz finds the long coat a staple of literature that conjured up anarchist tropes, announcing 'the shadowy figure of the black trench coat-wearing bomb thrower' embodying 'fears of disorder, social instability and threat' to democratic values.[2] Indeed, as Shantz points out, the first 'red scare' in the United States directed at anarchist labour organizers made use of the shadowy figure in a dark trench coat—a Russian threat—to announce the spread of communism and anarchism. Anarchists summed up the threat from within, one enabled by foreign forces, thus the capacious coat stood in for fears of subterranean movements intent on overthrowing the established order.

In literature, the anarchist combined military know-how with an apparent disregard for law and order, possessing the survival instincts of an unauthorized military actor. Alongside their capacity for secrecy, anarchists were painted as figures actively working against democratic values. Following a terrorist act, the undercover anarchist could proceed to blend with the local population. Never mind the reality that anarchists were, historically, less likely to engage in violent acts than other insurgents, the image was potent in post-war American society. Images of conspirators finding cover for their identity under a black coat goes as far back as C.K. Chesterton's 1908 novel *The Man Who Was Thursday,* where the anarchist character is illustrated through observations of his attire. Replete with internal threats not observable to the naked eye, the man in the capacious dark-coloured coat went on to give material form to social and political upheaval. Manifest in the image of the anarchist anonymously walking the streets with dynamite in his pockets, the man-in-trench-coat was assembled from the fears of an excess of democracy. Regarded as nihilists and terrorists, threats to the status quo were typically clothed in a cryptic cloak encoding deep-seated fears and anxieties. Threats were everywhere, but in literature they took on a decidedly masculine and urbane form. Featuring strongly in imperial narratives from late-Victorian and Edwardian literature, the anarchist-in-trench-coat trope contained the sneering assumption that insurgents were enabled by the supposed privileges cosmopolitan modernity bestows.

In the Edwardian metropolis, various internal threats tormented the establishment, so perhaps it is not surprising to find the quotidian trench coat surface in James Joyce's novel *Ulysses*. Set in early twentieth century Dublin, Joyce's alternative vision of social life recreates the ordinary and everyday as epic; thus the trench coat arrives in the form of the character Macintosh, who, following his first appearance at the funeral of Paddy Dignam, is known simply as M'Intosh.[3] A tragic, shadowy figure, he bears all the signs of a man suffering a modern malaise, mourning a lost love, suffering some form of insanity, and driven to eating dry bread.[4] Named after a coat with a reputation for troublesome odours, M'Intosh is a shadowy figure. Trench coats accompany uncertain journeys, lending anonymity to the solitary male figure moving through the city. Paul Fussell suggests that of the surviving portmanteau words from the First World War (amongst them *trenchknife* and *trenchfoot*) *trenchcoat* took on a life of its own.[5] Trench coats conveyed war-weariness and dislocation; neither heroes, nor cowards, ghostly figures dressed in the dark mantle were in search of a place in the world. Was the man-in-trench-coat a proxy for the war wounded, a symbol for the empty, hollow survival of those who returned from the trenches? Or was this figure a cipher for the disenchantment of post-war society? The threat of another world war, a modernity based on colonialism and extractive industries, internal class conflicts and the slow break-down of old hierarchies were all threatening the status quo. A solitary embattled trench-coated male figure emerged as a loaded symbol to comprehend various complex transformations.

As Celia Marshik argues, literature of the 1910s, 1920s, and 1930s emphasized the trench coat's connotations of violence and anonymity, reflecting 'a profound disquiet about the way bodies were imprinted by forces beyond their control'.[6] In modernist literature, the significance of the trench coat narrates troubled bodies and disturbing relationalities at work. Literary work mined the potential to explore these subtle and tortuous realities through new embodied states, attitudes, and styles. Virginia Woolf and James Joyce found in the trench coat a locus for social changes that were upending old certainties. Unsettled by gender and social class inequalities, this period saw the establishment weather challenges from suffragettes and labour organizers. Meanwhile the anti-colonial imagination was in full flight. Revolution, anti-colonial struggle, and challenges to old hierarchies had a certain inevitability following the First World War. As William Butler Yeats in his 1919 poem 'The Second Coming' warned, 'the centre cannot hold'.[7] A line written contemplating revolutionary action in Russia and Ireland, he laid bare the ills of modernity in his tortured reflections on lost innocence and the hollowing out of humanity. For Yeats, everything was falling apart, seen in his despair that 'Mere anarchy is loosed upon the world,' no doubt a reference to Ireland, which was by this time changing beyond all recognition.

Turncoats

1919 was a decisive year in Ireland's history. The December 1918 election saw the Republican party Sinn Féin win a landslide victory, followed by a refusal to take their seats in the UK Parliament, after which they proceeded to set up their own separate parliament known as Dáil Éireann (meaning Assembly of Ireland). Thereafter they declared Irish independence, created a provisional constitution, and reaffirmed the 1916 proclamation of the Irish Republic. January 1919 coincided with the start of the Irish War of Independence; the year Yeats wrote the chilling line admonishing the hysterical desire for upheaval:

The best lack all conviction, while the worst
Are full of passionate intensity.[8]

Ireland was not the only place where the cracks were showing; the aftermath of the First World War had created new countries in Europe and the Middle East, dividing and displacing minority ethnic groups, a carve-up that would create tensions for decades. As boundaries were redrawn, millions of Europeans were placed in a minority situation within newly created territories. For Ireland, the war had been an opportunity to stage an uprising in Dublin in 1916; Irish Volunteers and the Irish Citizen Army seized the General Post Office and other key sites in Dublin to declare an Irish Republic. Despite the failures of the Rising, the UK government response to execute the leaders of the rebellion garnered sympathy for the insurgents and loosened the hold the imperial centre had over Irish people.

By the time Dáil Éireann was in place and the War of Independence had begun, the Volunteers were largely known as the Irish Republican Army (IRA). The distinctive trench coat was, from 1919, the garment of choice for the guerrilla leaders in the conflict (also worn by the Crown Forces). Their experience (as the Irish Volunteers) improvising weaponry and clothing in the 1916 Rising found them ready to equip themselves for insurgent action, best achieved through asymmetrical warfare, camouflage, and subterfuge. By this time, they had a more systematic and streamlined approach to military operation, relying largely on the co-operation of

Irish citizens to compensate for their limited resources against the British Crown forces. A sort of 'uniform' developed—a favourite of the 'flying columns' in the countryside—consisting of 'a dark jacket, a collared shirt, riding breeches, leather gaiters and boots, a Sam Browne belt, bandolier, belted trench coat, and soft cloth cap'.[9] Trench coats—outdoor, gritty, practical—confirmed the IRA as figures of action, in contrast to the suited administrators prepared to make grubby compromises with the British Crown. Tom Barry, commander of the 3rd West Cork Flying Column, described the mismatched uniforms of his comrades, 'Their boots and leggings were muddy, their trench-coats hung open, no collars adorned their necks'.[10]

Connotations of violence and anonymity, first surfacing in anarchist tropes, and then in literature, found expression in the trench-coated bodies of insurgents acting against the imperial centre. For a group searching for an identifying symbol, 'the trenchcoat was the epitome of dash among the guerrillas'.[11] It also summed up the disquiet felt about bodies imprinted by alien forces. Troubled bodies were forging new styles of being, at the edge of Europe, in outfits that confirmed they would unsettle old certainties. Michael Collins, a larger-than-life figure of the period, nicknamed 'The Big Fellow,' co-ordinated attacks on police and British intelligence agents in Ireland. In 1919, Collins contacted Ned Broy, a British police detective who had turned spy for the fledgling government. At the time, Broy had heard much about Collins, but not having seen a photograph of him prior to the meeting was struck by the guerrilla commander's appearance 'dressed in black leggings, green breeches and a trench coat'.[12] Everything was falling apart, but largely people were placing their faith in the shadowy figures of the revolution, who fashioned a uniform from the remnants of war and distant memories of the trouble that anarchists and outsiders had caused the British establishment.

To evade the gaze of the enemy, insurgents were driven to adopt a uniform with shape-shifting qualities, concocting modes of self-presentation that could mobilize destruction, but would not give them away on the streets and in the fields. Low-level conflict involves temporary, incomplete, and constantly changing spatial organization, reflected in the transformations that guerrillas underwent to stay ahead of a powerful enemy. By 1920 Ernie O'Malley, an IRA officer, was leading battalions in the countryside and amongst his memories of winter he described 'a heavy trench coat which clung to my back and sides with rain, sweat or heavy misery, my clothes splashed with mud and water'.[13] Later in the year he feared the trench coat was making him a target from his own side, since the Auxiliaries (a paramilitary unit of the Royal Irish Constabulary) wore similar coats: 'They heard me moving up the road and had seen my tin hat and the shape of my trench coat against the sky,' when he realized that 'they had taken me for a British officer and were ready to fire,' before he was recognized and could go on his way.[14]

Irish literature came to seize upon the trench coat as a symbol of the conflict, in particular its evocation of stealthy presences roaming the countryside. Elizabeth Bowen's novel *The Last September* has an unsettling reminder of the changing shape of Ireland in the form of a mysterious trench-coated presence. Set in 1920, the young Lois Farquar from an Anglo-Irish family witnesses a strange sound in the countryside, a dark ghostly form discernible only from the sound of the imposter's outer-garment: 'The trench-coat rustled across the path ahead, to the swing of a steady walker,' causing her to wonder, 'It must be because of Ireland he was in such a hurry.'[15] Once back at home she remains silent about the episode, lest her family would not understand or believe her story. For Lois, the sound was unmistakeable. Trench coats stood in for hidden dangers and shadowy presences in the conflict.

Irish theatre, too, referenced the sartorial choices of the rebels in the later Civil War that saw different factions turn against one another in dispute over the Treaty compromise. *Juno and the Paycock*—a play from the Dublin Trilogy by Sean O'Casey—revolves around the trials and tribulations of a Dublin family amid the Civil War. Theatre critic Gabriel Fallon suggests those who first saw the play in 1924 would have felt the desired frisson when Boyle, a leading character, upon hearing a noise, furtively peers out the window and says to the family gathered inside, 'It's a fellah in a trench-coat.'[16] Early audiences of the play understood exactly what this meant.

Fallon was convinced that the trench-coat 'became "the battle-dress of the IRA,"' recounting that, 'Many a peace-loving citizen—myself and Sean O'Casey included—affected a trench-coat, only to find oneself the object of

FIGURE 7 Dublin 1922. Anti-Treaty members of the Irish Republican Army (IRA) in Grafton Street, Dublin during the Irish Civil War. (Photo by Walshe / Getty Images).

suspicion from more than the forces of the British crown.'[17] Resembling working men in civilian clothes, save for the gun grasped close to the body, the image induced terror because it had a double-face; as such, guerrillas could relish their unauthorized civilian-combatant status. Combining the menace of the terrorist with the casual heroism of the citizen-soldier, they repurposed the garb of the army officer in a fight against the Crown; all the while making use of the trench coat's camouflage, its practical mobility, and the cover it gave to weaponry. A figure of romance, the gunman on the run who (by any means necessary) sought to destroy British rule in Ireland, was summed up by the spectre of the 'fellah in a trench-coat,' a figure that for Peter Costello represented for the Anglo-Irish at the time, including W.B. Yeats, the 'return of evil into paradise'.[18]

Women were, of course, amongst the republican insurgents threatening the status quo in 1920s Ireland. A photograph of female IRA scouts reveals the same garb, including the practical, all-purpose trench coat, the perfect shield against the rain and a capacious cover to conceal weaponry. In the snapshot, one of the IRA scouts is seen with an ammunition belt wrapped around the waist of her double-breasted coat, bearing the storm flap (what some call the 'gun flap'). Carrying Lee Enfield rifles, the women wear an assortment of headgear, a scene that confirms a unit ready for violent skirmishes in the Irish countryside.[19] In these troubled times, the trench coat-clad figure was a symbol of romantic nationalism and heroic resistance, but (as the fictional Boyle family from the O'Casey play knew) they had a certain menace. The image of the rebel was also attractive to young would-be recruits. Writer Frank O'Connor—who signed up to be given the 'safe' job of carrying dispatches, scouting, and trenching roads—was first attracted to the cause by the sight of 'young rebels slouched around in trench coats with hats cocked over one eye'.[20] Romantic idealism and the prospect of a fight summed up the allure of this casual militarism. O' Connor recalls scraping up essential equipment and, 'In the absence of proper uniform our Army tended to wear riding breeches, gaiters, a trench coat, and a soft hat.'[21] Tellingly, he muses that the period of political unrest was a safety valve, for him and for the country, going on to explain that 'the Irish nation and myself were both engaged in an elaborate process of improvisation.'[22] The putsch was improvised and the costume followed suit. Trench coats, amongst other essentials, could be picked up anywhere, instantly endowing recruits with the required rebellious attitude. Instant access to such wild adventures attracted the young and rootless from small towns and the rural lower middle-classes, who made up the rank-and-file of the IRA.[23] A distinctive part of the ensemble, the old, battered war-worn trench coat made it into the folklore of the revolution. Later it featured in a popular Irish rebel song, the 'Broad Black Brimmer,' installing the garment into popular memory of resistance:

It's just a broad, black brimmer
Its ribbons frayed and torn
By the carelessness of many's the mountain breeze
An old trench coat that's all battle-stained and worn
And britches almost threadbare at the knees…[24]

Casual Heroism

For historian Gavin Foster, the 'trench coat is the most iconic component of the IRA ensemble' in this period and into the

Civil War that followed.[25] First worn by First World War officers in the 1910s, into the next decade the IRA were attracted by the practicality of the trench coat for modern combat, which included large pockets to store manuals and maps.

Its weatherproof qualities came into their own in a country known for wet weather, to hide guns and ammunition, but also to keep them dry, making the trench coat the perfect accessory for guerrillas whose distinctive brand of warfare atomized military action. A light, water-repellent covering gave volunteers mobility, but also made them indistinguishable from other civilians or the Crown forces, since by this time the trench coat was widely available to purchase. During questioning following his arrest by the Auxiliaries, Ernie O'Malley was asked, 'Where did you get the officer's trench coat? At Macroom? Stole it from a dead man, of course,' to which he replied that he bought it in a shop, before noticing the name of a Dublin outfitter on the label, giving his captors reason to link him to an IRA operation in the capital.[26] Trench coats were everywhere; they were visible on the streets and sold in shops, but were quickly gaining a deadly local significance. The exchange between O'Malley and British Auxiliaries reveals the extent to which the First World War had militarized civil society in Britain and Ireland. Anti-colonial struggle exploited the confusion, making trench coats a sign of larger fissures forming in the body politic.

Irish romantic-realist painter Seán Keating embellished the myth of the trench-coated warrior taking on the Crown with his painting *Men of the South*, depicting one of the IRA 'flying columns' set within the Irish landscape. Based on the artist's sketches and photographs of members of the secret guerrilla column, the North Cork Brigade, Keating had them sit for the portrait in 1921 during a period of ceasefire in the War of Independence, holding guns and wearing the trench coats and soft caps so favoured by the guerrillas.[27] When they arrived at the Dublin Metropolitan School of Art where Keating was working, the porter shocked by the sight of armed men in the distinctive garb of the IRA, and it took some reassurance from the artist for the man to believe that their presence posed no danger.[28] A mixture of live sittings and compositional photographs allowed Keating to complete the painting. First shown in 1922, *Men of the South* was one of a series by Keating that bore witness to the gritty reality of this period of unrest in Ireland. According to Éimear O'Connor, the absence of Seán Moylan—leader of the column—from the painting reveal the risks involved in depicting the men too faithfully, given the activities of the column at the time.[29] The painting bears witness to the conflict in ways that align heroism with risk, made plain by the dishevelled looks and improvised uniforms of the subjects. Battered trench coats, a distinctive part of the military costume immortalized in Keating's painting, consign regimental attire to the past, and in doing so, create a new kind of political imaginary.

Giving form to a version of military heroism that somehow embodies the fight, improvised uniforms were shaped by the spatial features of anti-colonial struggle.

This new kind of soldier hero—complete with bandoliers casually resting over battered trench coats—embodies not the sovereign gentlemanly state, but its rupture. To combine the most efficient qualities of the regular soldier with the anarchist, the guerrilla had to be equivocal about uniform. If invisibility was critical to guerrilla action, then at certain opportune moments the body of the insurgent was destined to come into view. Rebels emerged in the garb of the IRA, a costume with enough flexibility to transform and mutate at a moment's notice. And yet, despite the bravado, the painting also conveys the fragility of its subjects: youthful excitement, yes, but also the sense that these men had propelled themselves into a future beyond their control.

The prominence of the trench coat in the War of Independence and the subsequent Civil War, worn by various state and non-state actors in the conflict, reflects the blurred boundaries between war and peace. Is this the first instance of insurgents adopting the uniform of the other side? Did the Irish insurgents discover the deadly potential in fusing civilian and military styles of being? The trench coat bears witness to the recoil from the First World War, its excess, which had a habit of spilling over into other conflicts. Modern insurgencies tested the potential for mobilizing untrained, fragile bodies, leading them to improvise a path to some unknown future. Memories of the trench-coated freedom fighters were, however, not always generous. By the 1960s, Irish poet Thomas Kinsella in 'A Country Walk' describes his disillusionment with the transition from revolution to independence, contrasting romantic Irish nationalism with what he regarded as the petty materialism of independent Ireland. The rebellious energy of bygone days and the greedy capitalism that replaced it, struck him as equally ludicrous, causing him to reflect that the revolutionaries:

> …have exchanged, A trenchcoat playground
> For a gombeen jungle.[30]

Incomplete worlds and disappointing outcomes haunt the poem, painting both the conflict and its aftermath as absurd versions of juvenile frolics. More ludicrous perhaps, is the sight of aging rebels embodying the spirit of rebellion in ill-fitting clothes of a lost era. A notable veteran of the Civil War, Dan Breen, appears in a 1928 photograph in a leather trench coat that sits awkwardly on what was by this time his podgy middle-aged figure.[31] If the trench coat had political significance to the memory of Republican resistance, afterwards it was a rare sight in Irish political life, its currency spent in a conflict that cost human life and realigned loyalties. For future generations it left a legacy of heroism, but it was also remote, a memorial to extraordinary times and the brutality of extra-parliamentary politics. Trench coats returned in fashionable form in later decades, having lost their association with the events of that violent period in Ireland, when this subversive uniform (improvised from the remnants of past wars) was given vicious new life against its inventors.

5 REPORTAGE

Trench Coat Prose

An American reporter stands on the steps of an Amsterdam conference hall. He fastens up his trench coat against the heavily rainfall. People gather outside, anxious for updates from the peace conference taking place inside. A shot is heard in the crowd. A diplomat has been assassinated, placing our reporter in a live news story. John Jones' first assignment in Europe proves to be quite an escapade. He travels under an assumed name, proceeds to get embroiled in a series of encounters with villains and spies, uncovers a conspiracy, survives an attempt on his life and a plane crash, witnesses the outbreak of war, and falls in love. Alfred Hitchcock's *Foreign Correspondent* (1940) follows the travails of the quintessential reporter: passionate, anti-intellectual, intuitive, and relentlessly in pursuit of the story. In the final scene, Jones (Joel McCrea) broadcasts his story from London—in the Second World War—while bombs fall around him, warning Americans to 'hang on to your lights; they're only lights left in the world'. Along the way he loses his trench coat, but Jones' physical presence embodies the reputed 'foreign correspondent,' a figure willing to venture beyond his comfort zone, displaying reckless disregard for the dangers lurking 'out there'. Part truth and part fiction, the mythical trench-coated reporter lasted for at least another forty years.

Reporters may not always have worn trench coats, but the civilian-combatant style story suited many. The myth was potent in newspaper rooms. Sent by the *Baltimore Afro-American Newspaper* to report on Black Americans volunteering for the International Brigades in the Spanish Civil War, Harlem poet Langston Hughes returned sensational dispatches. Reporting from 1937 Madrid he wrote home to say, 'It's a thrilling and poetic place to be at the moment.'[1] Hughes wondered whether he would live long in the midst of conflict, but as a biographer notes, 'not to make himself out to be a hero, he allowed himself only now and then to write true *trenchcoat prose*'.[2] Shorthand for danger and recklessness, excitement and intrigue, the curious epithet 'trenchcoat prose' described the sensational writings of adventurers and daredevils. It differentiated them from the majority daunted by the prospect of breaching domestic borders. Hughes travelled to Russia, Cuba, Haiti, France, and Japan encountering war, civil unrest, and revolution, deepening his craft along the way. His was an intellectual journey to venture beyond the boundaries of home in search of new ways of being.

Trench coats held a certain romance for adventurers, but also for those who looked on, too fearful to make the journey. Insurgents and renegades wore them, as did writers, intellectuals and correspondents who sought to live on the edge. But in the 1930s and 1940s, it was also clear that the trench coat was the uniform for a variety of actors in and around the field of battle. This included combatants of the International Brigades. After the Spanish Civil War, some of those exiled to France formed the Spanish Maquis group and went on to fight against the Franco regime until the early 1960s. A fearsome reputation arose due to their repeated sabotage of infrastructure, violent robberies, and assassinations. Photographs reveal insurgents carrying improvised weapons in quasi-uniforms fashioned from everyday working clothes. Trench coats surface in photographs of the Spanish Maquis from France and Spain.

During the Civil war itself, accounts suggest that Quico Sabaté—known by his comrades as 'El Quico'—had a reputation for pulling a Thompson submachine gun from under his raincoat in various guerrilla actions.[3] Sabaté, fought on the Aragon front in the Spanish Civil War, but was exiled to France where he became involved in the Maquis resistance to the Vichy regime. After the Second World War he returned to continue insurgent activities against Francoist Spain; an intriguing 1955 photograph reveals Sabaté wearing a trench coat in Barcelona with his homemade mortar, 'looking for all the world like some sort of international spy'.[4] Credited with inventing this mortar to throw anti-Franco leaflets from buildings and taxis, Sabaté, like many anarchists, found in the trench coat a cover for guerrilla actions. Hiding 'El Quico's' gun and miscellaneous tools to sabotage Franco's regime (and Vichy France), the capacious coat was an ordinary but effective mode of resistance.

If trench coats stood in for the fears particular regimes had about their ever-weakening authority, in some cases it was true. In Sabaté they found its all too real embodiment; a quick-witted operator given to swift and decisive actions who was prepared to pull weapons out from under his coat. His trench-coated body conveyed all the menace of a man who was violent and ruthless, but rarely came into view. It was the pace and the energy of insurgency that drove rebels to improvise uniforms, and the trench coat authorized an unpolished and unmediated violent image that militant separatists occupied in the first half of the twentieth century. Moving in and out of view, rebels chose the trench coat as a cover, but it was also light enough to carry with handy pockets for field maps.

For the establishment the trench coat was troublesome. As Hughes' 'trenchcoat prose' suggests, stories of bravery, violence, and danger were bound up with images of volunteers bravely facing dangers for which they were sparsely prepared. In the Irish Civil War, the Spanish Civil War, and other conflicts, trench coats became part of the kit of various insurgents. As asymmetrical warfare drove rebels underground, the trench coat—part military, part civilian— offered the ultimate disguise.

War-Worn

American writer Ernest Hemingway did not originate from the edges of society but was determined to occupy them. A careful balancing act saw him craft a persona befitting a man of letters, but he was also searching for an image novel enough to announce a new era. Brutality and violence had characterized the birth of the new century, which might have triggered his search for modes of being that referenced violence and, more importantly, its survival. This drove Hemingway's experiments with military clothing following his return from the war, which included a *Spagnoli* uniform he had specially tailored (a uniform only worn by Italian army officers, not Red Cross volunteers as he had been), which constituted his first act in a life fashioning himself as war veteran. Military clothes, part of a conscious effort to boast war experience, held a certain romance, but the regalia was not quite right and, according to Marilyn Elkins, it was not long before he graduated to trench coats and khakis.[5] His advice, writing in Toronto's *Star* in the 1920s, to men seeking to contrive a military past, was telling:

A good plan is to go to one of the stores handling secondhand army goods and purchase yourself a trench coat. A trench coat worn in winter time is a better advertisement of military service than an M.C. If you cannot get a trench coat buy a pair of army shoes. They will convince everyone you meet on a street car that you have seen service…[6]

His candour is striking. To feign a military past, he advocates nothing more elaborate than a trip to the shop, a quick fix to fabricate a back story. Not content with mere military styling, his ruse was to urge men to wear something with enough dirty material integrity that it could persuade any passer-by of war weariness, and no better way to authenticate barely achieved military experience than to get into the clothes. Not regalia that proclaimed military experience, but down-at-heel combat gear that quietly whispers, 'this is a man who has *seen action*, but does not wish to talk about it'.

For Hemingway the trench coat was a good costume—neither too fancy nor too transparently military—to accompany him throughout his life. Hemingway was adept at crafting an outsider image assembled from myths of physically durable men. 'Papa,' as he liked to be called, was a fan of bullfights and rugged adventure, and this image confirms one of the motifs of his life and literature, namely the outward appearance of fearlessness and the comradery of men. He rejects the trappings of dress uniform in favour of the pared-down authenticity of the war-worn trench coat. As style briefings on the trench coat might say, his look is 'effortless'. He swops standard male status symbols for a natural, rugged physicality that says *I don't care*, despite clearly crafting a look with as much care and precision as his writing. This masculine under-dressing consisted of 'military khakis, hunting vests, flannel shirts, sweater and trench coats,' a calculated minimalism that rejects gentlemanly conformity, passivity or any hint of femininity.[7] Hemingway understood the modern male hero and imagined that this is what he might look like. Dressed in a costume that was unmistakeably there but did not to draw too much attention to itself, his masculine look was engineered to be enigmatic, yet always implied action. His sartorial choices were so prescient that they would endure in the form of army surplus, sports clothing, and streetwear into the latter part of the century.

Covering the Spanish Civil War for the American Newspaper Alliance, and arriving a year after it started, Hemingway made sure he packed a trench coat. His time in Spain, reporting on the conflict and travelling through the country, inspired his novel *For Whom the Bell Tolls*, and here he is found (following his own earlier advice) wearing a trench coat. The travelling companion of many who covered war and catastrophe in the golden era before the Second World War, 'when foreign correspondents travelled fast and light in well-worn trenchcoats,' the look was a growing trend for a certain type of man.[8] This was the heyday of swashbuckling correspondents—partly there for a job, partly for the fight—when 'the best of the bunch tended to be self-trained and self-promoting.'[9] This perhaps accounts for a 1937 photograph of a trench-coated Hemingway, pictured sitting alongside Soviet filmmaker Roman Karmen, and Dutch filmmaker Joris Ivens, somewhere in Spain.[10] Karmen, a film reporter during the Spanish Civil War, highlighted the Republican cause in documentary films that fused the 'live report' with intellectual montage. In the photograph the three men stare intently at the camera in a somewhat distracted state. Karmen and Hemingway sport Basque berets and trench coats, both symbols of rugged male adventure in the 1930s, a second skin for men who wanted to blend with the chaos. But the writer's beret also appropriates signifiers of separatist militarism, perfecting Hemingway's rebellious mix-and-match costume. He authenticates military experience, while skilfully avoiding the conformist connotations of uniform.

FIGURE 8 Left to right: Roman Karmen, Ernest Hemingway and camera operator Ioris Iveno. Spain, 18 September 1937. SPUTNIK / Alamy.

Hemingway in Spain is captured in another photograph, this time his brush with death in 1937, alongside Ivens, standing between the camera and a black sedan riddled with bullet holes.[11] A scene of devastation reveals the visibly relieved faces of the passengers, Hemingway and Ivens, who managed to hop out of the car just in time. We find the writer barely maintaining his composure next to the wreck; the camera captures a tense moment, 'his hands safe in the pockets of a long tan trench coat that is partly buttoned, its collar turned up against the cold'.[12] Ivens had reportedly politicized Hemingway and converted him to anti-fascism, having introduced him to all the right people in Spain. The International Brigades were chock full of men that held an appeal for Hemingway—intellectual, tough, and vigorous— and he would come to admire the authenticity of their risk-taking masculinity. His trench coat was living up to its potential. It was the travelling companion that made sense of the life he wanted, getting him as close as possible to the action.

Alienation and Survival

Hemingway's work exerted considerable influence on twentieth-century ideals of manliness. His 1926 novel *The Sun Also Rises*, based loosely on his own experiences, retrieves the reputation of post-war men—from dissolute to resilient—

through his protagonist Jake Barnes, who gets entangled in dramas that test his manhood. A search for inner integrity animates the story of the American in 1920s Paris and Spain, whose masculinity is not a given, but is nonetheless achieved against all odds through painful processes of self-making. Costuming reflects Hemingway's interest in the process of crafting the self against a hostile external world in clothes that announce defiance, strength, durability, and vigour. Seeking out distinctly masculine adventures, Hemingway combined strenuous pursuits, such as outdoor sports and hunting, with heavy drinking. His quest for the deep integrity he perceived in men caught up in war—embattled by inner conflicts—became the subject of his stories. Self-making was at the heart of his masculine ideal. Having been in and around various conflicts as a volunteer or newspaper correspondent, military adventure was a defining feature of his literature and life. In the conflict he found a locus for the existential conflicts of men, and while he lionized the man of action, he was more concerned with internal struggles that emerge in war—for him, the true primitive feelings that surface in the face of brutality.

A distinctly masculine individualism was embodied in his choice of clothing, but the image of an embattled trench-coated Hemingway reflected his insistence that manhood was forged in a struggle with forces beyond his control. His Spanish adventure was newsworthy and extended his reputation for bravery and politically charged causes. Acutely aware of an audience, he populated the Hemingway legend with sensational photographs of his hunting adventures, battlefield experiences, and sought the company of adventurous edgy men. Clothing helped to build the persona of war veteran, sportsman, adventurer, and tortured artist. His military reputation might have been forged in his experience in the First World War, but the legend perhaps masked the fact that in Italy he had served with the American Red Cross, rather than any military unit. Military clothing was a lifelong obsession, that found him wearing 'the trenchcoat and khakis that returned veterans adopted,' a conceit that feigned military experience to complete the Hemingway look.[13]

Living vicariously through the trench coat gave him an enlarged biography, as if he could rewrite his own life by simply trying on various costumes. In summer 1939, Hemingway made a visit to the Sun Valley Resort in Idaho in the US, part of the Wood River Valley, a place he would frequent for the next twenty years, often with celebrity guests on hunting and fishing trips. Lloyd Arnold's book, illustrated with his own photographs, is filled with images of his friend 'Papa,' cataloguing hunting exploits and good times spent there with friends and family, but also includes a passage to illustrate Hemingway's sartorial habits. One morning he rose early from bed and, 'threw on a trench coat over his pyjamas and robe' to bid the hunting party farewell before returning to a day of writing.[14] For Elkins, clothes embodied his unique style of machismo, a sense of 'cool' that told its own story about Hemingway's desire to live on the edge.[15]

It captured the thrill of getting into scrapes and surviving them. A carefully crafted persona rejected worldly trappings, but paradoxically was achieved by furnishing his life with material things, such as military clothing. His life was full of objects—notably, guns—to support the fiction of a man casually withdrawn from the materialism of American life. Two of his homes, kept intact for posterity—one in Key West, Florida, and another in Havana, Cuba—reveal a finely tuned taste for eighteenth-century antiques, antelope heads, and modernist paintings. Objects were enlisted to disguise his immersion in the hum-drum acquisitiveness that constituted the hellish all-American dream. His dream was an escape from his social origins, to eschew gentlemanly propriety and to swop the prospect of suburban mundanity for a more primal and cerebral existence.

Outdoor sports and hunting, heavy drinking, comradery, politics, were all part of Hemingway the artist and man. His trench coat embodied the persona. A.E. Hotchner's biography of Hemingway gives an impression of the writer in later life clinging to the costumes of his younger self with an image of 'Ernest wrapped in his big trench coat' at the races in Paris in 1950.[16] When he stopped in the town of Burgos in Spain in 1954 (to visit the cathedral), Hemingway 'stood for a moment at a side alter, looking up at the candles, his grey trench coat, white whiskers and steel-rimmed glasses giving him a monkish quality'.[17] Moccasins and a worn trench coat denote lost adventures, capturing an image of the star writer having lost his once youthful exuberance. In his quest for an authentic sense of self, 'Papa' Hemingway's trench coat was with him to the end of his life. In a critical passage of his novel *Garden of Eden,* the protagonist David wears an old trench coat to walk out of his hotel into the rain, a cover for anguish (the fracture showing in his relationship with his wife Catherine) as he faces into an unknown future.[18] As literary symbol, the trench coat acts as cover against psychic pain.

For Hemingway the trench coat might have been a weak membrane against psychic threats, a thin disguise in a hostile world, but it was also defiant. A second skin, the trench coat intensifies the image of a world without limits, armour for the unending battle against hidden dangers the world holds for men. Considering its place in literature, film and popular culture following the war, it comes to signal the threats that lie just beyond the knowable world. Following the Second World War, this feeling of alienation intensified, to coincide with the trench coat's growing reputation as the garment of choice for white men, ostensibly to furnish a narrative strand of alienation and survival. This theme I will return to later. A tortuous version of masculinity, given visual potency by trench-coated men at war was given expression in civilian life by adventurers, risk-takers, and truth-tellers. This was Hemingway's universe. Howard R. Wolf recalls a longing to adopt the mantle of the foreign correspondent, to use language as Hemingway had done:

I wanted to become a foreign correspondent and to wear a Burberry trench coat as soon as I learned that Hemingway had been sent overseas by the Toronto Star. I didn't know if he wore one, but I assumed he did, and the tragic photo of him walking 'in the woods near his home in Ketchum in the final winter of his life' suggests that I was right.[19]

Without any previous evidence, Wolf had been convinced that the American novelist was likely to have worn a trench coat, and this photograph finally confirmed it, just as he had imagined. Fantasy and reality start to blur. Hemingway's story suggests that the trench coat was by the end of the Second World War gaining significance as symbol of a new kind of masculine style, a whole manner of being, a loose mix of militarism, adventure, travel, and outdoor sports. But it was more than that. Trench-coated men were veterans, not just of a contained battle, but of life changing experiences that threatened to spill out into civil society. This opened the door to the fantasy of a private, self-contained, moral man with enough courage and potency to resolve the eternal problem of how to face the outside world with confidence.

How could the inner self be protected against corruption unless there was an outer membrane that said 'no, you cannot cross'? Part of the mythical kit for the foreign correspondent, the guys in 'well-worn trenchcoats' held a certain allure.[20] American journalist and broadcaster, the late Walter Cronkite recalls 'the model of the newspaper reporter' as a glamorous figure whose 'mandatory costume reeks of wartime experience—the trenchcoat with its vestigial epaulets'.[21] It was a key part of late Canadian American reporter Peter Jennings's travelling wardrobe. Fellow journalist Hilary Brown confirms that his 'very glamorous life overseas' was in part an image cultivated to convey an appetite for adventure and a dogged determination to seek out truth, and so 'he looked the part. Of course, he had a beautiful trench coat and a very nice battered briefcase'.[22] Jennings travelled widely to Vietnam, Hungary, East Germany, Romania, South Africa, and various parts of the Middle East, reporting from conflict zones and gaining a reputation for getting very close to the story. Practical, war worn, drab, knowing, but also a mark of civilized composure, the trench coat told its own truth.

Hemingway's masculine malaise found in the trench coat a gendered object to act out all the anger and disappointment of a post-war return to normality that could never happen. And yet, the image of Hemingway at the end of his life is not inconsistent with the traumatized anti-heroes of his novels: battered, ill, isolated, and poor, they wander through the city trying to make sense of their surroundings. Trench coats and battered suitcases together form a powerful image of thwarted heroics. By attempting to repair their inner conflicts with maladaptive behaviours, they confirmed the image of the dissolute trench-coated man as cipher for a war-ravaged, alienated masculinity. Such dissolute styles of being were permitted. Status claims made by the trench coat can feel hollow and provisional, but as the image solidifies in American culture following war, it describes the retreat from settled forms of masculine privilege. Cloaking violent, desperate secrets and desires, the trench coat adorns embattled heroes hiding in plain sight. As the next chapter shows, the myth undergoes an intensive churn in literature and film and finds the trench coat flourish as a symbol of decay and alienation in post-war modernity.

6 HEROES OR VILLAINS

Shadowy Figures

A young woman, disillusioned with the cruelties and deprivations of her life in a bleak port town, longs to escape. Only her luminous trench coat signals a desire for a better future. Illuminated by the bright, shiny coat, she holds out hope against the gloomy backdrop of the foggy, shadowy port. In contrast to the surrounding atmosphere of dodgy dealings and menacing characters, her optimistic appearance is a shallow attempt at survival. As the narrative unfolds, all glimpses of hope for Nelly are shattered. A film in French poetic realist cinema, Marcel Carné's *Port of Shadows* (1938) is set in Le Havre, where army deserter Jean (Jean Gabin) first encounters Nelly (Michèle Morgan). Dark but reaching for the light, trench coats enter the unsettled atmosphere of the 1930s and 1940s. Their implied truth is that there is no truth, just a constellation of barely comprehensible episodes, actions, and moods. Enigmatic and malleable, the trench coat takes on the dubious role of heroic symbol in a world of anti-heroes, misunderstood outsiders, and villains.

Trench coats come into their own in a cycle of crime films popular in this period. As much part of film noir as the dark, rain-soaked streets, hard-boiled detectives, and looming city skylines, trench coats intensify the sense of confinement so familiar to these narratives. Coined by French film critics just after the Second World War, the term 'film noir' described a provocative American crime film known for violent eroticism and hard-hitting themes.[1] A style rather than a genre, film noir derives its visual codes—primarily stark contrasts—from German expressionist cinema. Characteristics of the noir style include the male detective, the femme fatale, a central enigmatic event, followed by a suspenseful narrative infused with a sense of foreboding. Visual codes make it instantly recognizable, but distinctive sartorial elements—the trench coat (with fedora) in particular—constitute its most recognizable elements. Set against a backdrop of Depression, Prohibition, and a changing policing landscape, the noir style painted the enemies of law and order (and their enforcers) in broad strokes. Portraying what writer Raymond Chandler described as the 'mean streets' of US cities, detective fiction made the problem of criminality—and its containment—a focus of the action. Alongside scientific policing and new discourses of 'deviance,' urban crime became a matter of public interest, giving the detective an enlarged role in resolving dilemmas, real and symbolic, for a society seeking redemption from larger upheavals.

Trench coats signal a mood change in Otto Preminger's film noir *Laura* (1944), from the bright lights of New York's Manhattan to the dark clouds forming overhead. As the plot darkens, a Madison Avenue executive, Laura Hunt (Gene Tierney), thought to have been murdered in her fashionable apartment, becomes the focus of a police investigation. Manhattan police detective Mark McPherson (Dana Andrews) enters Laura's flat on a rainy night (in search of clues) in a trench coat. An air of suspicion surrounds the various characters in Laura's life, and one by one, they don the sinister coat. We follow the action through the eyes of the detective, whose growing obsession with the ghostly character of Laura is interrupted by her unexpected return. An optimistic, perky look is replaced by her dour trench coat, plunging Laura into the web of deceit contaminating her social circle. The trench coat renders all characters in the film suspect, but also hints at sordid passions and drives that lie beneath cool, polite exteriors; we are given to believe that nothing is as it appears.

It is perhaps no surprise to find the figure of the detective—white and male—set a normative standard for who could enforce order in film noir and crime fiction. But there was an added dimension to the detective's typical make-up, namely a determination to seek out and uncover truth, bringing a (supposedly) disinterested eye to the disorder of city space. This was not just an American problem. Paramilitarism had reached its heyday globally in the first half of the twentieth-century, given the complex range of nationalist and revolutionary forms of violence emerging, which led to the entanglement of politics and security in various regions. Renegade behaviour by unofficial groups was growing, as was the paramilitarizing of homeland security, giving rise to groups with 'nebulous identities (even if they were official): whether they were dressed in civilian or military gear (or a blend)'.[2] According to Uğur Ümit Üngör, paramilitary groups could be bottom-up enterprises or state creations, but all shared the characteristic of 'politics in the demi-monde,' a position exploited to authorize corruption and violence.[3] The Balkans, Ireland, Germany, and China (amongst others) all saw paramilitary structures shape politics and social life in the first half of the century. Crime fiction in 1930s America reflected the anxieties that these boundary transgressions—between military and civilian, between banditry and policing—generated, and the threat that an illicit, ever-present underworld posed. In many ways, crime fiction did the imaginative work, comprehending and disentangling appearances from reality in this layered, opaque environment. Trench-coated characters emerged to resolve dilemmas created by duplicitous appearances in urban America.

Reality cannot be taken as given in a world where law-makers, law-enforcers, and law- breakers are indistinguishable. This is played out in *Laura*, where trench coats stand in for suspicion of criminality, reflecting fears of an environment so opaque that the expected signifiers of violence are barely discernible. It was not ordinary crime that concerned crime fiction, or the noir films that followed, but organized crime, with its origins in a grubby politics that blurred boundaries between state and non-state violence. 'Nebulous identity' reflects the paranoia surrounding sartorial representations of underworld characters.[4] Their specific kind of menace was directly proportionate to the lack of certainty people had about their loyalties. Fascination with the gangster image, though, derives from the fear this kind of coercive power could instil in onlookers. A thoroughly ambivalent character, the screen gangster seemingly cultivated an aggressive masculine image but also displayed sartorial flamboyance.[5] Clothes reflected their subversive behaviours, the mere sight of which terrified a public who were nonetheless flocking to movie theatres to see them on screen.

The toxic mix of fear and desire these characters aroused was unmistakeable. When made in Hollywood studios, film noir and other crime-related movies became subject to the 1934 Hays Production Code, which regulated depictions of crime, violence, and sex up until the 1950s. Illegal or immoral behaviour had to be punished on screen, giving prominence to a cycle of noir crime films.[6] Preferring the movies to promote social aspiration and conformity rather than narcissism and indulgence, reformers sought to control content. Films such as *The Maltese Falcon* (1941), *Murder My Sweet* (1944), and *Gilda* (1946) came under scrutiny as film noir managed to survive the Code. Part of what Ula Lukszo calls the 'consumable characteristics of noir,' dress codes played down the glamour of the gangster; they could manage the problem, as it were, by employing a set of conventions with their own logic.[7] A constrained atmosphere saw cinematic crime take on a more psychological aspect, pushing filmmakers to find ways around the Code with ambiguity and artistry.[8] Trench coats were part of this trend to play with cinematic conventions, giving filmmakers scope to covertly reference violence and suggestive scenarios through dramas of revelation and concealment. Various pleasures and horrors could conceivably be lurking underneath a trench coat.

Humphrey Bogart was perhaps the most famous film actor to wear the trench coat (repeatedly). He did more than many actors to embody the new American screen type, 'the ethical rebel loner,' whose depiction of Sam Spade in *The Maltese Falcon* affirmed that this type of man was made to survive with stoicism and style.[9] In Michael Curtiz's *Casablanca* (1942), he plays Rick Blaine, an American nightclub owner with a shady past forced to choose between love and country. Blaine decides against joining Ilsa Lund (Ingrid Bergman) in a single heroic gesture for the war effort, making the closing scene of the film one of the most iconic in American cinematic history. Blaine in a trench coat and Lund in a stylish suit stand on a foggy airport runway saying goodbye to their longed-for future together. This film scene might have done more than any other to make the trench coat a stand-in for loss, longing, and tough self-sacrificing masculinity against the backdrop of the Second World War. Evolving into a symbol for collective effort (the Allies) rather than isolationism

(US first), sacrifice rather than indulgence, in *Casablanca* the trench coat is aligned with official values that the US sought to promote during the Second World War.[10] Yet Blaine's choice is his alone, reflected in the sovereignty the trench coat affords him. So too, another Second World War drama, *The Key* (1958) finds Sophia Loren's agonizing situation reflected in images of her body wrapped tightly in a trench coat, positing survival as the outcome of self-reflective acts of moral courage. Individual rather than collective discipline shaped various conformist narratives of survival during wartime, making the trench coat a symbol of autonomy.

Trench coats in film work well to convey the ambivalent attitudes of characters forced to exist in unsettled spaces, where the reliability of visual perception itself is put in question. Set in post-war Vienna, Carol Reed's *The Third Man* (1949) amplifies an atmosphere of distrust and suspicion through a disorientating visual style (including the 'Dutch Angle' camera) that presents Vienna as troubled territory. Harry Lime (Orson Welles) at the centre of the action is a vivid illustration of the evils of individualism (a racketeer) at a time of crisis. Autonomy might be the key to salvation, but—if abused—can be the path to ruin. Major Calloway (Trevor Howard) in his black trench coat, a figure of military authority, looks like he alone can bring order out of the chaos. As the camera moves through labyrinthine spaces haunted by shadowy presences, silhouettes become critical to the narrative. Viewers are given a choice between two modes of

FIGURE 9 American actor Humphrey Bogart (1899–1957) in the 1940s. (Photo by Pictorial Parade / Archive Photos / Getty Images).

survival: the bureaucratic order of Calloway or the unofficial and turbulent world of Lime.

Nothing is at it appears when trench-coated figures appear on the horizon. Cinematic depictions found the sartorial symbol reflecting multiple narratives, corporeal states, and moral positions. The proud autonomy it affords characters like Blaine does little for women, often acting as a sign of loose morals or hopeless outcomes. Robert Aldrich's *Kiss Me Deadly* (1955) opens with a barefoot woman running frantically along a dark road in nothing but a trench coat. She gets into a car, driven by a private investigator, but she cannot quite catch her breath. As the car drives away, her prolonged gasping lingers just a little too long, taking on sexual overtones as jazz plays on the radio. Did the trope of the sexy woman with nothing underneath her trench coat draw on this arresting opening sequence? Was she rescued just in time? A trench-coated woman conveys a troubling and morally dubious mode of autonomy, a scary aberration. In reaching for autonomy, she is painted as a temptress losing her grip on reality, rather than taking control of it, giving the trench coat an entirely different kind of texture on a woman's body, a cue for loss of control, sexual perversity, and danger.

By the 1950s, the Hays Code was no longer viable. As the trench coat symbol embedded in the cinematic lexicon, the garment detached from good-versus-evil scenarios. Liberated from convention, trench coats retain their sense of mystery, but in film were free to represent more dissolute and complex states. Even when the trench coat is calculated

FIGURE 10 Kay Francis, American actress, 1934–35. Taken from Meet the Film Stars, by Seton Margrave. (London, 1934–35). (Photo by The Print Collector / Print Collector / Getty Images).

to titillate, it is an ideal diversionary tactic. Brigitte Bardot's trench coat in *Babette Goes to War* (1959) is a comical take on wartime subterfuge, but its playful things-are-not-as-they-seem dramatic potential also surfaces in Marilyn Monroe's last film, *Let's Make Love* (1960). Worn by Catherine Deneuve in *Belle de Jour* (1967), the patent black trench coat (designed by Yves Saint Laurent) suggests insecurities and inner turmoil but primarily acts as a cover for repressed sexual desire. Mobilized time and again to titillate, to indicate risk and subterfuge and to denote hidden insecurities, whether overt or covert, the trench coat in film had many faces. In the cinema, trench coats invited audiences to abandon fond illusions and settle into an inherently unreliable universe.

Containment

The fictional detective Philip Marlowe is one of the most resonant trench-coated figures of American crime fiction. A creation of Raymond Chandler, Marlowe is the inspiration for many subsequent tales of the sleuth moving through the city on a dangerous quest. In *The Big Sleep*, a 1939 novel set in Los Angeles in the Great Depression, Marlowe's assignment is to investigate the attempted blackmail of Mr. Sternwood, a wealthy man in failing health. It was later adapted by Howard Hughes for a film of the same name, *The Big Sleep* (1946). In the book, the detective's journey leads him into a series of encounters with the man's wayward daughters, with the dark recesses of the city and with various shady characters from the criminal underworld.

During his investigation, Marlowe navigates the sordid spaces of 1930s Los Angeles, witnessing bribery, illegal gambling, and murder. A streetwise air and cool exterior bely the complexity of his task: to separate fantasy from reality in a sphere where nothing is as it appears. He has access to the police, but also to the killers and racketeers of the city, moving between them with skill and cunning. His watchful, self-sufficient persona is on show when we find Marlowe sitting in his car outside Arthur Geiger's store on a rainy night: 'I struggled into a trench coat and made a dash for the nearest drugstore and bought myself a pint of whisky. Back in the car I used enough of it to keep warm and interested.'[11] We witness him moving between worlds, from the Sternwood mansion to Eddie Mars' gambling joint, from LA diners to Geiger's store, which he uncovers as a pornographic lending library.

Marlowe has the ideal vantage point from which to unearth LA's secrets. Trench coats, heavy rain, dark interiors, and incessant smoking screen the true motivations of characters. Marlowe's masculinity is predicated on extreme watchfulness (waiting and following suspects), a talent for giving very little away (one liners replace conversation), a complete absence of greed (he will not take his fee), and an avoidance of romantic entanglements (both Sternwood sisters are promptly rejected). Women present a danger to the hard-boiled detective, either because they distract him from his quest, or they threaten to ensnare him in the degeneracy of the city. A fixer and man of action, Marlowe's trench coat intensifies his defensive, tough image, a metaphor for his resistance to criminality, but also to seductive women and the corrupting influence of dark money. When he finds Carmen Sternwood at a crime scene intoxicated and naked, he recognizes her as a victim of sexual exploitation and does the right thing—considering his client is her father—and acts quickly to get her out. His fastidiousness is on display: 'I went over to the divan and peeled off my trench coat and pawed through the girl's clothes,' but once he gets her dressed, he quickly pockets the evidence, locks the desk, grabs the keys, and puts his coat back on to leave.[12] Chandler's Marlowe has presence of mind even in the most extreme circumstances.

On one level, this is an old-fashioned tale of tug-of-war between good and evil, but on the other it encapsulates the dilemmas of a post-war America reeling from the shocks of war and the Great Depression. For film scholar Stanley Orr, the story is not all it seems, revealing colonial undertones that link the moral purpose of Marlowe's quest to his anxious determination to bring savagery under control in semi-tropical California.[13] Placing his work of separating and cleansing in a wider context, Orr reveals Marlowe's place in a larger scheme as he '*wraps* himself in the archetypal trenchcoat and similarly *swathes* the toxic Carmen' for fear of going native in a city painted by Chandler as replete with foreign bodies, orientalist interiors and fallen women.[14] The narrative aligns the gangsterism of LA with strange foreign objects, such as a totem pole, Chinese embroidered clothes, and characters with 'mad eyes'. To get the situation under control, Marlowe's task of 'boundary-maintenance' gives the 'cohering trenchcoat' a role in fortifying his body against the threat of primitive forces.[15] His quest goes beyond scientific policing. With his trench coat, Marlowe performs a purifying ritual as he extricates himself—and shields Carmen—from the sordid surroundings.

Getting the house in order, as it were, involves resisting temptation; to keep it together, his trench coat (at least on a symbolic level) distances him from dangerous others threatening to contaminate his quest, to block his destiny. He must remain impervious. Once again, the trench coat signals unease about insides and outsides, self and other.[16] The cryptic coat is a metaphor for the quest; on the surface to solve the mystery of the blackmailer, but ultimately, to disentangle mysteries, to separate good from evil. Women (when they are available) plunge Marlowe into an anxious state, which suggests that 'Marlowe's notion of masculinity utterly depends on hermeticism, on remaining free from this contagion.'[17] A trench coat seals him off from harm, acting as a protective shield to render his body impervious to alien influences.

When he returns to his apartment to find Carmen waiting in his bed—staging an awkward seduction attempt—his response is not curiosity, but anger. Seeing 'some jungle emotion' in Carmen's eyes and infuriated by the imprint she leaves in his bed, evidence of 'her small corrupt body still on the sheets,' he 'tore the bed to pieces savagely'.[18] In Hughes' film, Marlowe is similarly incorruptible but lacks the tortuous ambiguity of Chandler's incarnation— impermeable, yes, but more comfortable in his skin. In common with many detectives in the noir style, he acts as a mobile observing post, his eyes revealing 'distinct modalities of urban anxiety' that follow the unsettling circuits and rhythms of the modern city.[19] Trench-coated men, fashionable women, and flamboyant gangsters set the scene for a drama that enacts the restoration of order by male authority figures.

Sartorial symbols serve to maintain male fraternity and power; they mark bodies to denote continence (trench-coated men) and excess (women, criminals, and foreigners). In conversation with Captain Gregory, Chandler's Marlowe hears how the police captain views the job: 'Being a copper I like to see the law win. I'd like to see the flashy well-dressed mugs like Eddie Mars spoiling their manicures in the rock quarry at Folsom.'[20] Good and evil are pitted against each other so that (real) men can take their place as the guardians of law and order. Effeminate 'well-dressed mugs,' on the other hand, are a threat, ready to destabilize the carefully balanced order of things. Shot through the man-in-trench coat image is the desire for an archetype, a figure to perform purifying rituals to cleanse the streets, to bring truths to light, and to disentangle insiders from outsiders. Official figures wear trench coats to denote their retreat from sartorial flamboyance and indulgent behaviour, work that demands a protective shield, to parry probing eyes and elaborate manipulations. Marlowe cannot be porous, but neither can his armour; a trench coat safely seals him off from a dubious world of shape-shifting characters.

FIGURE 11 THE CHEAP DETECTIVE, 1978 Peter Falk. © Photo by: Colombia Pictures/Ronald Grant/Everett Collection.

The noir look did away with the gangster film by professionalizing the protagonist, upgrading him to moral adventurer, as tough as the gangsters, but whiter, more masculine, and better educated. Embodied by a trench-coated Bogart, this repurposed screen Marlowe—via Blaine—would become a resonant symbol of American masculinity. Such was the popularity of Bogart's characters that parodies, such as Woody Allen's *Play it again, Sam* (1972) and Robert Moore's *The Cheap Detective* (1978), later send up the noir formula referencing key cinematic moments including foggy terminals, heart-wrenching goodbyes, and of course, trench coats.

7 OUTSIDERS

Angst and Duplicity

A singer lives out an embattled existence in war-ravaged Berlin. The Second World War has just ended; she has nothing left but her intellect, her allure, and a few surviving possessions, including a trench coat. Billy Wilder's dark comedy *A Foreign Affair* (1948) tells the story of a love triangle in post-war Berlin, where Republican congresswoman Phoebe Frost (Jean Arthur) is a visiting rapporteur observing the war-devastation of the city. When she finds an underworld of profiteering and dark goings-on, her attention quickly focuses on German singer Erica Von Schlutow (Marlene Dietrich). Suspected by Frost of involvement with high-ranking Nazis, she pursues Von Schlutow in the hope of locating her associates. What follows is a story of intrigue and savage survival—the trench coat highlights the distinct versions of femininity the women represent. When Von Schlutow is captured following a raid on the club where she sings, she grabs a dark trench coat to cover her glamorous stage costume, a different kind of masquerade. Von Schlutow's trench coat disguises her stage persona, itself another layer in the masquerade, this time erotic femininity.

Frost, the interloper with only a shawl pulled over her evening dress, has no cover. A sign of her inability to fortify herself against the threats of this sordid, semi-militarized environment, her lack of armour is laid bare, and her meddlesome naivety is reduced to a bad joke. Frost's saviour fantasies are at odds with her surroundings. There is a moment when she borrows an army trench coat from Captain John Pringle (John Lund), but it sits uneasily, as if compromising her in some way. Unlike Marlowe, the moral purpose of her quest is undercut by her *lack* of cunning, set against the ease with which the worldly Von Schlutow can occupy multiple realms. Here, the trench coat disguise temporarily seals her from harm before the singer slips back into her stage persona once again.

The demand to fortify the self against unseen dangers gave the trench coat a place in film and literature as equivocation conditioned real people's lives. Noir film is reflective of 'angst, apathy, war-time paranoia' and anxieties about masculinity during and after the war.[1] Marlowe's barely concealed colonial quest comes out of the shadows with the emergence of a new kind of detective in Cold War dramas. These reactionary characters unashamedly targeted outsiders. *Dragnet*, an American TV series that ran through the 1950s and 1960s, depicts Sergeant Joe Friday (Jack Webb) moving through Los Angeles driven by a sense of outrage about the various threats in his midst, shamelessly seeking out criminality in

FIGURE 12 Eine Auswaertige Affaere, Foreign Affair, A, Eine Auswaertige Affaere, A Foreign Affair with Marlene Dietrich, Jean Arthur. 1948. (Photo by FilmPublicityArchive/United Archives via Getty Images).

the subcultures of post-war America. Friday's trench coat was by this time a key symbol in the 'television incarnation of the paranoid style in American Politics' where 'the "other" is omnipresent'.[2] Friday updates the self-imposed exile of the trench-coated detective but is much more knowing. Owing something to the noir style of masculinity, the show's sparse style and Friday's tenacity make sense of his ruthless quest to pursue subversives, reflected in his insistence that witnesses stick to the facts, without embellishment.

FIGURE 13 DRAGNET, Jack Webb, (1966) (1967–70). Photo: Thal/TV Guide/Courtesy Everettt Collection.

Friday bends the rules in pursuit of his heroic quest, determined to restore normality in a narrative dominated by a sense that he is disentangling appearances from reality. Luc Boltanski argues that the structure of detective fiction implies truth is not easily apprehended, that law cannot protect the state from subversion, so that 'maintaining order implies suspending or sidestepping the law, resorting to a regime of *exception*'.[3] If the detective genre places the protagonist on the boundary between public and private spheres, then the drama spotlights this zone as the fulcrum for the restoration of trust.[4] Venturing into the realm of exception that Boltanski identifies, Friday's task is to restore order to the margins, assembled as he is from the Chandler-esque figure of the hard-boiled detective. It becomes clear (especially in the second run of the series) that the dissolute and ambiguous detective figure is wholly rehabilitated to seek out and punish various 'symbols of social upheaval' identifying 'hippies, protestors, pot smokers, black militants, liberal intellectuals,' as potential state enemies.[5] In 2002, Donald Rumsfeld's Pentagon briefing identified, in true right-wing fashion, 'known unknowns' as the greatest threat to US security. Known unknowns were Friday's targets: threats are everywhere but hidden, cannot be identified but must be pursued. Fear of the unknown brought anxieties to the fore that sought to justify the expansion of a regime of exception, a Cold War discourse that gave license to all kinds of semi-official transgressions. Friday's 'instincts' for uncovering threats were dubious, to say the least. But as he hunts down outsiders he mimics them—disguising himself as a subversive—resorting to a 'regime of exception' on the basis that sedition is ubiquitous, unseen but nonetheless an existential threat that needs eliminating. The message is chilling.

As the detective genre meets ideological agendas of the mid-century, the roll call of deviants and state enemies is enlarged to give the man-in-trench-coat a whole new significance. Such license paved the way for trench coats to take on a thoroughly ruthless image, seen in Alain Delon's portrayal of an assassin in *Le Samouraï* (1967), where a fastidiously buttoned-up and belted trench coat distances him from his brutal deeds. As trench coats gained a reputation for ruthlessness, they became the stuff of myth, exemplified by Ellie Driver's (Daryl Hannah) trompe-l'oeil trench coat in *Kill Bill* (2003), a twenty-first century pastiche of the assassin's uniform.

The trench coat did not decline with the changing face of social struggles depicted in film but continued to adorn outsiders forced to go undercover. In Jean-Luc Godard's French New Wave film *Alphaville* (1965), the trench coat amplifies the sense of trepidation the protagonist feels in facing an expedition into the unknown. It seals off Lemmy Caution (Eddie Constantine) from ever-present temptations and entanglements as he pursues the enigma of Alpha 60. Lest he get sucked into the logic of this forbidding techno-dystopia, Caution's sacred mantle accompanies his investigation of the fascist computer creation. A trench-coated persona is pitted against the technocratic villainy of the computer's lab-coated inventors in a drama that goes beyond good versus evil to take on the tyranny of soulless scientific invention. In a similar vein, Ridley Scott's *Bladerunner* (1982) finds Rick Deckard (Harrison Ford)—a former cop-in-trench-coat—tracking down bio-engineered human replicants in a fictional 2019 Los Angeles. There he encounters Rachael (Sean Young) in full neo-noir style, dressed in a 1940s skirt suit and furs, who he suspects is a replicant. In a film where nothing is as it seems, *Bladerunner*'s dress code revisits the paranoia of 1940s noir with a posthuman flavour. Where loss of identity and purpose in the post-war American male might have been embodied by the trench coat and fedora, here noir dress codes are enlisted to grapple with a different set of questions concerning verisimilitude in the 'nature' of human presence itself.

To romanticize Deckard's quest, the voice-over is hard-boiled, 'delivered by a protagonist whose trench coat seems to have been lifted from Orson Welles in The Third Man'.[6] Cybernetic capitalism is presented as a new dilemma with roots in older problems, a contagion that bears the imprints of governing institutions. Like the gangsters of old, the replicants can no longer be controlled and the authorities regard them as a threat. Deckard, enlisted to terminate rogue replicants, is an unwilling arm of the law, since—in keeping with the noir myth—he realizes that the quest lacks moral authority. A science-fiction narrative resonates with problems that plagued the post-war western world, ravaged by

FIGURE 14 Harrison Ford in a scene from film Bladerunner (1982). (Stanley Bielecki Movie Collection / Getty Images).

corporate greed, built on imperial extraction, and sustained by war. A smoky, noirish atmosphere paints a picture of an urban wasteland feeling the heat of climate crisis and ravaged by environmental vandalism. We follow the protagonist to unearth corruption so horrific that it goes to the heart of society itself.[7] War-weary, alienated, overwhelmed but still in possession of a moral core, Deckard in his trench coat gives *Bladerunner* its own brand of romanticism, painting the protagonist as a beacon of hope in the smoky, opaque wastelands of the future.

A claustrophobic atmosphere where decentred humans wearily battle through illegible cityscapes and labyrinthine spaces haunted by shadowy presences confirm the modes of survival available in the postmodern-posthuman world. But even in this sci-fi future, trench coats articulate ever-more defensive modes of survival that affirm individual sovereignty as the only safe position from which to navigate a complex world. Denis Villeneuve's *Bladerunner 2049* (2017) has K (Ryan Gosling) tracking down androids thirty years later to 'retire' them as he moves through dystopian cityscapes, ravaged landscapes, post-industrial shelters, and the wastelands of Los Angeles. In a (faux) fur-lined dark trench coat, his hero's quest is given a futuristic shield updated with reinforced panels (and no doubt high performance techno-textiles), protecting him from the choking atmosphere of climate change. In his coat pocket hides a wooden horse, a childhood 'memory' that holds out hope of his humanity in a synthetic life-sphere.

Artificiality is brought to the fore to convey the same sense of bleak posthuman authoritarianism washing the soul out of life-worlds. K eventually encounters an ageing Rick Deckard (Harrison Ford) frayed by the downward spiral of society, its corruption more prevalent than before, as it enters a deeply sinister phrase. Searching for humanity (he 'dreams of cheese'), his environment has been compromised beyond his imaginings and survival–for both detectives– pushes him to isolate from others. Doubt consumes K as he disentangles the seen from the unseen, the artificial from the real, finding no reprieve from his embattled existence in an authoritarian dystopia. Thwarted heroics, embodied by his trench-coated image, reveal the pretensions of earlier adventures into the unknown and the futility of the lone quest. A quest of another kind in Ron Howard's *Solo: A Star Wars Story* (2018) follows the story of Han Solo (Alden Ehrenreich) who teams up with Tobias Beckett (Woody Harrelson), Chewbacca, and others in an intergalactic adventure that tests friendship between outsiders. In a futuristic trench coat, Beckett morphs throughout the film, from good guy to bad guy, good bad guy to bad good guy. Solo first meets Beckett on the battlefields of Mimban (with helmets, armour and trench coats inspired by First World War movies) posing as an Imperial officer to later be revealed as an intergalactic criminal. Beckett's ambivalent position has the perfect cover in a trench coat; it sees him through various trials and tribulations all the while concealing his true allegiances (which are constantly changing). His sage advice to Solo, his key lesson for survival, is to trust no one, since 'everyone will betray you,' revealing his position as a shrewd operator living on the margins. Neither a villain nor a hero, unencumbered by morality or loyalty, Beckett survives with style and resilience. However decentred the universe, formidable the enemy, or illegible the landscape, Beckett has one constant. Upholstered and encased by the mythical coat, he can move in and out of various positions, navigate the dangerous labyrinthine spaces of the galaxy, and emerge intact.

Intellectual Autonomy

Albert Camus wore a trench coat throughout the 1950s until his untimely death in 1960. In 'sharp gangster suits underneath a trench coat' he was such a convincing image of the noir outsider that, when he visited the Vogue offices in 1946 for an interview, the office staff described him as 'a young Bogart'.[8] Existential cool was given form in Camus' style choices, which embodied instinctual self-creation centred on individual acts of moral courage.[9] An image of stoicism and a retreat into subjective reality, the trench-coated existentialist expressed a style of autonomy that sought dignity in the containment of the self. Defensive modes of survival fashioned individual sovereignty to shape the intellectual-as-outsider image. Symbolic protection against the various assaults on intellectuals, trench coats constituted a 'cool' retreat from worldly trappings, itself a mechanism for 'masking inarticulate rage'.[10] The darkness implied by trench coat-wearing was largely a masculine conceit, but women writers were also attracted to their symbolic potential to express defiance against prevailing tyrannies.

Henry Miller's trench coat was a staple of the American playwright's wardrobe. Countless images reveal writer William Borroughs sporting a belted trench coat look. When Man Ray photographed Pablo Picasso in 1933, the artist chose a trench coat for the sitting; a mix of intensity and self-contained confidence affirms the aptness of the garment for projecting autonomy.[11] If they gave intellectuals a sense of independence, then images of Simone de Beauvoir, Guy Debord, and Gilles Deleuze shrouded in trench coats illustrate their attempts to locate a sartorial symbol that would position them as detached observers. Science-fiction writer Michael Moorcock remembers late 1940s and 1950s London as 'noir-ish times, when every young man desired nothing much more than a trenchcoat and a battered fedora,' describing a burgeoning literary scene that reflected the prevailing atmosphere of grumbling disenchantment.[12] With imperial myths dead, blitzed London provided the backdrop for bittersweet romanticism, reflected in plays of the so-called Angry Young Men, and the melancholia of poets such as Philip Larkin (whose bitterness bore the faint echoes of a hoped-for future cruelly thwarted). Writers of Moorcock's vintage set the noir myth against another, more promising science-fiction world. Weighing up the options, he describes his dilemma: 'For half my youth I yearned to be riding some strange complaining reptilian steed across the dead sea bottoms of Mars while for the other half I longed to be wearing a trench coat, a snap-brim fedora and walking the rain-sodden streets of the big city.'[13] Tired myths of imperial masculine adventure were set against a new and more capacious version of otherworldly escape. If science fiction fantasies set up alternative worlds, then mythical noir figures kept returning to the past. Doomed to the eternal puzzle, the noir figure was left with the futile task of trying to separate the good guys from the bad buys.

A peculiarly white kind of melancholia was expressed in the thwarted heroics of trench-coated figures. Taking on a whole new texture when worn by Black post-war writers, such as James Baldwin, the trench coat reached beyond narratives of imperial longing. Alienation of a different type is captured in a photograph of Baldwin in 1960 walking down a Paris Street, in conversation with modernist painter Beauford Delaney, both dressed in trench coats.[14] Having first met in New York twenty years previously, they formed a friendship through the bohemian circles in which they moved, where Delaney introduced the young Baldwin to jazz and painted portraits of him. When Baldwin left the United States for Paris, disillusioned with racism, Delaney pursued exile five years later. Following Delaney's death, Baldwin remembered him as an example of 'absolute integrity: I saw him shaken many times, and I lived to see him broken, but

I never saw him bow'.[15] Pain, exile and defiance pervade his memory of Delaney, a fellow artist with whom he found comradery. Trench coats cohere against anxiety, but they also anticipate violence, a weak defence against a hostile world; still, their shape-shifting qualities might have warded off the dangers of domination and division. A shield to mask drives, passions, and allegiances came into its own at a time when surveillance was on the increase. For intellectuals this was an ever-present danger: a trench coat was a symbolic defence against the threat of dehumanization.

French Philosopher Michael Foucault announced his retreat from the dehumanizing effects of a disciplinary society with a trench coat. In 1966, the *L'Express* newsweekly declared Foucault the most important thinker since Jean-Paul Sartre in a review of his publication of *Les Mots et les Choses* translated into English in 1970 as *The Order of Things*, with a headline 'The Greatest Revolution Since Existentialism'.[16] To confirm his revolutionary potential, a three-quarter page photograph of Foucault (above the headline) reveals the intellectual in a trench coat, wearing thick spectacles and a knowing smile. His bold position, according to reviewer Madeleine Chapsal, was to 'announce the excellent news: the death of Man'.[17] Freedom and liberty is called into question by the young Foucault, who critiqued the constraining forces of systems and objects he identified as constituting the cruel web created to trap people in a dehumanizing existence.

According to Foucault, human experience was organized and limited by the structures promising freedom and enlightenment, such as medicine and education (later Foucault would also write about prisons). By blowing apart old certainties, his study of the human sciences revealed an oppressive nightmare of systems created to strangle us. For him, they would execute our ultimate undoing through the very things we were given to believe were the markers of civilization and hope. We return to the agency of objects and the hollow words we use to describe them; we see broken people wearily putting on old military coats to brave the elements, to face hidden enemies, as if by donning a second skin they might ameliorate the threats inherent in every interaction and assault lying in wait. For Foucault the trench coat was no protection at all; but by wearing one he perhaps offered a timely reminder that civil society—with its imaginary guarantees—might be our fondest illusion.

8 STYLE

Equivocation

A detective emerges from the subway in a brown leather trench coat and proceeds to walk through the busy New York streets. The camera surveys the city from various angles: at street level, from above, through cracks in buildings. The detective occupies the centre of the action, meeting acquaintances, hailing a taxi, surveying the scene. So far, so familiar, but this detective story represented something new. The first movie in the detective genre to feature a Black protagonist, Gordon Parks' *Shaft* (1971) features John Shaft (Richard Roundtree) hired by a gang boss to locate his kidnapped daughter, leading him into fighting factions of the criminal underworld. Shaft is out on his own in his distinctive polo necks, tweed suits, and long leather trench coats. Like many film detectives that came before him, Shaft has extraordinary access to various groups in the city and can anticipate trouble: he talks to the police but does not trust them; he has contacts in both the Black Panthers and the gangs. Like *Bullitt* (1968) and *Klute* (1971), *Shaft* has a paranoid edge featuring strong autonomous types apparently forced to deviate from standard procedure. As the voiceover for the trailer announces, John Shaft is 'Hotter than Bond, Cooler than Bullit'. Shaft is competent, even-handed, has access and is equipped with a wardrobe that 'represents his equivocal social position'.[1]

FIGURE 15 SHAFT, Richard Roundtree, 1971, walking past the Apollo Theatre, New York. Courtesy Everett Collection.

Gordon Parks, the first Black director to make a major Hollywood studio film, established his name as a photographer and, like Shaft, was fond of a dapper trench coat. Photographs show Parks at work clutching his camera wearing 'what would become a signature piece for him: the well-worn trench coat'.[2] Parks covered sports, theatre, racial segregation, and poverty for US magazines, but was a fashion photographer for a significant part of his career at *Life* and *Vogue*. Parks saw in the trench coat a means to tell stories about survival, understanding that this sartorial symbol went a long way to convey just how self-contained the modern protagonist had to be. Roundtree admits that 'the character of John Shaft, if truth be known, was Gordon Parks,' recalling Parks' interest in getting the look exactly right.[3] Criticized at the time as Blaxploitation—a commodification of Blackness—the film's sartorial style likely caused detractors to recoil from the movie. But as Roundtree commented a year later, Shaft's character wardrobe held a certain magic for filmgoers. Recalling a visit to a high school in Washington DC, he describes how schoolkids would run around to the side door to get closer to the actor, 'grabbing at my leather coat. They wanted to take it!'[4] Shaft's appearance was a large part of the appeal of the film, and Roundtree's time as a fashion model might also have given him a sense of how to inhabit the clothes, conforming to while at the same time subverting archetypal men's styles. Parks and Roundtree understood fashion—*Shaft* tells a larger story about empowerment through sartorial style, and in doing so, crafted a mainstream film that went against the grain.

As cover for various struggles and transformations, the trench coat has acted as a mode of disentanglement. In the late 1970s, with the death of Mao Zedong and the end of the Cultural Revolution, China underwent a period of reform, and by 1978, the release of Japanese film *Manhunt* (1976) starring Takakura Ken inspired new clothing styles in China.[5] Singer Mou Xuanpu recalled the impact of the crime drama on his wardrobe: 'I bought a trench coat (*fengyi*) and dark glasses to look like [Takakura] and grew my hair … I remember that trench coat looked great. I saw it for sale in Wangfujing and brought it straight away.'[6] One of a whole host of styles that signalled China's changing political landscape in the 1970s, the sartorial statement made cultural transformation visible and corporeal. In late 1970s China, trench coats and sunglasses introduced an element of darkness and mystery into a sartorial system that had, during the Cultural Revolution, been about illuminating the body, making it available to discourses of productive citizenship. Trench coats positioned bodies differently, as the look was cloaked and shrouded to suggest depth and intensity. New cultural flows into China—in the form of films and popular songs from Japan, Taiwan, and Europe—shaped a post-socialist China, but also reshaped attitudes to fashion and style. Along with women's new feminine fashions, men in trench coats re-sexualized popular culture and set the scene for mass consumer fashion.

FIGURE 16 The Trench Coat As Seen By Hardy Amies Around The 1960'S. UNITED KINGDOM. In A Street Of London, Five Trench Coats Of Different Colors Being Presented By The Friends Of Hardy Amies (Photo by Keystone-France/Gamma-Keystone via Getty Images).

A Time for Trench Coats

Holding its own during and after the First World War and gaining a decisive place in the Second World War, the trench coat evolved into a key emblem of twentieth century history. Its spread brought military uniform (albeit dressed down) into the realm of civilian fashion and style. Indeed, by 1952, *Vogue* (US) was reporting the 'return of the trench coat,' breathing a sigh of relief that its wartime role—in both world wars—had not consigned it to history, announcing its return 'in khaki-coloured poplin, with a lining of raspberry poplin' by Lawrence of London.[7] Regular comebacks and revivals are by now embedded in the trench coat narrative, which goes a bit like this:

> When clouds roll overhead, dig out a trench. The message seems to have been the unofficial mantra for designers this season as the British-born outerwear staple is once again everywhere, for women and for men. It makes sense. It always does. In terms of sartorial friends, you can't go too far wrong in taking up with a trench.[8]

Rather than consign the trench coat to the past, fashion's churn of styles and moods assists its routine reinvention. Academics might be intrigued by the ubiquity of modern technological designs such as the trench coat—its reach into various regions, its symbolic role in media and literary narratives—but the fashion industry has different agendas. At first glance, militarism and fashion might not be ideal bedfellows, but the utility and uniformity of military clothing has assigned it a place in the fashion lexicon.

Like denim jeans, the trench coat might be regarded part of the 'canon' of sartorial archetypes that, despite their resistance to change, have been embraced by the fashion system. Common sense, stability, reliability, and loyalty; hardly fashion attributes, but then again, the success of the trench coat owes much to the recent trend to invest in the 'heritage brand'. Big labels reinvent sartorial archetypes from their back catalogue, breathe new life into them with the help of their young designers, to raise the profile of the brand and realign it with a couture past. What Ornella Pistilli calls 'the heritage-creativity interplay' takes garments from the past to consolidate and recreate cultural imaginaries, consistent with the various ways in which 'fashion embraces history and images in its new formations'.[9] For fashion, the past resides in the present; cultural objects (from the past) materialize historical perception in sensual and immediate ways.[10] Fashion, as a symptom of modernity, reflects the ever-quickening pace of change set by metropolitan-capitalist energies.[11] This fast pace of change increasingly drives companies to mine the past for design inspiration, a reminder that fashion is a game of 'modernist irony'—a knowing unknowing— found in the reflective (and deflective) surfaces of the trench coat.[12]

A *Sunday Times* style journalist accounts for the trench coat's longevity: 'Like all the best fashion items, the trench started life as a practical piece,' but thanks to designers Alexander McQueen and Martin Margiela, has 'been reincarnated as the cover-up of choice'.[13] Such reinvention and *reincarnation* delights style writers, evidence of the heritage-creativity interplay at work. The options are seemingly endless as seen in Aimee Cho's 2006 line of trench coats 'that range from a timeless double-breasted trench to a "distressed" one that has metal in its cotton to make it wrinkly'.[14] From practical no-nonsense incarnations descending into various embellished and distressed states, trench coats are given the fashion treatment to birth multiple variations on a theme. But an air of mystery surrounding the trench coat sets it apart from other 'fashion staples'. They might be rooted in war stories, but trench coats have colonized whole ways of being in the last century (and a bit) from sleuths to war reporters, intellectuals to pop stars, city cops to style gurus.

Its romance was noticed early, and no doubt prompted Israel Myers, a Baltimore raincoat manufacturer, to set up the *London Fog* label in the early 1950s. He knew the garment well and was familiar with various technologies to achieve the impervious finish. He supplied American GIs with rubberized raincoats, and having seen Humphrey Bogart in *Casablanca*, he set about developing his own brand of trench coat.[15] As they eased into civilian life in the mid-century, trench coats were feminized to induce yet another incarnation. Yves Saint Laurent restyled trench coats for women in the early 1960s, consistent with his penchant for borrowing male dress codes to revitalize couture dressing. As second-wave feminism gripped the culture, the promise of the trench coat was an effortless, androgynous look, illustrated by a 1984 *New York Times* article, which described it as 'one of the first men's-wear styles to be adopted by women'.[16] Here, Greta Garbo, Marlene Dietrich and Katherine Hepburn are enlisted to convince readers of the trench coat's stylishly feminine qualities.

The trench coat's history is replete with gender anxieties. A 2004 *Vogue* (US) article promised 'androgynous allure will be amped up all the more if you throw a little feminine contrast into the mix,' as if the John Paul Gaultier trench might be a bit too manly for the fashion-conscious woman.[17] But for female fashion consumers, the trench coat is also touted as the perfect camouflage. A solution to 'whatever life throws at you,' trench coats are promoted as the accessory for the embattled woman, as a 2013 *Redbook* article attempts to prove by enlisting a range of celebrities to demonstrate its versatility.[18] To give weight to the claim, the article cites Audrey Hepburn's 'divine' trench-coated style, Tyra Banks' 'sex appeal,' and Kate Middleton's 'elegantly toasty' look.[19] You can be anything you want to be in this shape-shifting attire, or so the story goes. With trench coats, fashion consumers are offered just the right balance between freedom (to roam) and security (to be encased), a nod to earlier incarnations when it uniformed servicewomen.

FIGURE 17 BREAKFAST AT TIFFANY'S, Audrey Helburn and George Peppard, 1961. Courtesy Everett Collection.

The visibility/invisibility problem raises its head once again in the guise of trench coats that are either too elegant, too masculine, too fluid, or place too much pressure on women to be sexy. Sexual desires hiding under the trench coat—or presumed to be—recalls the noir film *Kiss Me Deadly* and the atmosphere of sexual violence that surrounded B-movies. These associations sparked a debate in 1970s Britain over a billboard advertising campaign for Gigi underwear. One billboard depicted a woman in a trench coat walking along an unlit street at night, staring fearfully at the camera. An image insert shows the same woman—this time averting her gaze—undoing her trench coat to reveal underwear underneath with a caption, 'Underneath they're all lovable in Gigi.'[20] Writer Rosalind Coward responded with an open letter to the British Advertising Standards Authority (ASA) with the retort, 'Underneath we're Angry,' exposing the adverts as sexist and demeaning.[21] Again, trench coats signify both danger and sanctuary, a place to hide or a garment to intrigue. Implicated in questions of identity, trench coats resist the demand to mark bodies as gendered, while also manipulating codes to signal sexual availability. Fashion features continue to regard the trench coat as a classic item or wardrobe staple. In other words, it never goes out of fashion. Complex cultural narratives have made the coat covetable, dangerous and cool, thus it holds a prestigious place in the fashion world. The garment offers sanctuary while bequeathing a sense of ownership and confidence, granting the suitably shielded citizen permission to move forward, to expose hidden parts of the self, to face uncertainty, or even to trespass.

In the language of fashion and style, trench coats are often bound up with conceptions of time. 'A Time for Trench Coats' from a 1990s issue of J Peterman catalogue returns to the origins of the coat, citing the digging escapades of squirrels, groundhogs, French Generals, New York famers, and English Kings.[22] J Peterman have a reputation for hyperbole, but when selling trench coats, they hardly need to reach for an expansive heritage. This is a garment with its own history. Time is key to comprehending the industrial discourse that first made this object meaningful beyond the military, in particular its facility to 'disembed' people from land. In a trench coat, human beings can be *on* the land without being *of* the land. Separating body from soil, the trench coat promises to assist our safe passage through unknown territory, following in the footsteps of the soldier, the war correspondent, or the detective. The trench coat plays tricks with time by apprehending the future through the past, and so it was with Burberry's venture into a digital future in 2009 when the company launched a website, 'Art of the Trench,' to engage consumers with the brand's legacy. Creative director Christopher Bailey said at the time, it's 'a way for our fans to interact with the culture of the brand and with the emotional aspects of the trenchcoat'.[23] By combining an archive charting the history of the coat with photo libraries for consumers to submit self-portraits wearing the legacy fashion item, heritage in fashion is revealed as a technique that demands emotional investment.[24] By 2016, the 'Art of the Trench' Middle Eastern campaign launched in Dubai, underlined the heritage message with a nostalgic return to origins by engaging 'craftswomen from Castleford, UK (where the iconic Burberry trenches are made)' who 'displayed their trench-making skills' at the event.[25] *Burberry* has lineage in trench coat making, and more importantly has found inventive ways to refashion the present by reaching into the past.

FIGURE 18 Poster advertising Burberry fashion house with Cara Delevingne in paper magazine from 2014. Advertisement, creative Burberry advert from 2010s.

Trench Coat Futures

Fashion assists time travel, and while trench coats can furnish a return to mythical origins, they also propel us into futuristic fabulations. Dystopian fashion in the recent work of designers Gareth Pugh, Demna Gvasalia, and Rick Owens have transformed the trench coat into a receptacle for new fears and anxieties, this time ethno-nationalism, plague, and climate crisis. Fashion evokes the dystopian mood with various structured garments (with a technological edge), amongst them PVC, sinister hoods, and military capes. If clothing announcing the end of days must come in regulation all-black, the leather trench coat stands out as the dystopian garment par excellence.

Black, leather trench coats are the garments of choice for *The Matrix* (1999), written and directed by the Wachowskis. One of the more influential amongst recent films visualizing imminent techno-dystopias, bodies have a curious role in the film, owing to the simulated reality that the Matrix represents, which saw protagonists manipulate physical laws to achieve their aims. Inspiring fashion collections and Cosplay costumes, *The Matrix* style is exemplified by the costumes of Neo, Trinity, and Morpheus. Conceived as urban camouflage to resist bullets, surveillance, and various physical threats, Morpheus' leather trench coat at first appears to be an update on the noir incarnation. As the film progresses it becomes clear that—along with Neo and Trinity—the heroic characters don trench coats to become majestic warriors, whose capacious coats elevate their status and helpfully conceal an armoury of

FIGURE 19 PRINCESS AURORA (aka ORORA GONGJU), Eom Jeong-hwa, 2005. © Cinema Service/ Courtesy Everett Collection.

FIGURE 20 FILM *THE MATRIX* BY ANDY AND LARRY WACHOWSKI. Keanu Reeves in the 1999 movie The Matrix. (Photo by Ronald Siemoneit/Sygma/Sygma via Getty Images).

weapons. With undertones of spiritual leadership, the black coats reach to the ground to affirm the characters as figures of redemption. Reminiscent of the frock worn by Jesuit priests (via Samurai movies) the black trench coats in *The Matrix* are a corrective to more conventional futuristic fantasies. Fans clamouring for the glossy leather coats can now find countless websites willing to offer a 'matrix leather coat selection'. If we were given to believe that all-in-one jumpsuits would be the regulation garment of the future, this movie suggests that the black trench coat is our true style destiny.

Afro-Futurism bends time (and space) by reinventing various garments, giving trench coats a cyber-punk edge, seen in Amsterdam-based label *Daily Paper*, whose FW19 collection included a green snakeskin belted trench coat with an iridescent quality reminiscent of a Matrix-inspired universe. So too this mix of African mysticism and technology transports us into another realm. Confrontational but completely in control, the contemporary trench coat embodies violence, but is enlisted to expose its structural roots. When singer Beyoncé wore a full-length trench coat for 'Ring the Alarm,' her scorned lover lyrics were overshadowed by the video's confrontational style—even more hard hitting at the 2006 MTV awards—painting an ugly picture of police harassment in twenty-first century America. Following a loud, aggressive siren call she bursts into action. In the video, her floor-length trench coat reveals leather shorts and thigh-high boots underneath, while uniformed police officers attempt (unsuccessfully) to restrain her. The parodic thrust of Beyoncé's trench coat exposes the police uniform as

FIGURE 21 2006 MTV Video Music Awards Show. Beyoncé performing 'Ring the Alarm' at Radio City Music Hall in New York City, New York, United States. (Photo by Jeff Kravitz / FilmMagic).

a sham surface, merely decorative veneer adorning a broken system. Style here is more than a surface effect; it uncovers a crisis of representation and the very real license that uniforms give to civilians. Her narrative suggests that if they, by virtue of their uniform, can trespass and authorize violence, then so can she. Beyoncé's propaganda feedback is a powerful instance of the utility of style stories to expose corruption, borrowing the regalia of the state to reveal how dubious these claims to power can be. Here, the trench coat, with its aptitude for shape-shifting and role-reversal, is enlisted to beat them at their own game.

CONCLUSION

Influencers arrive at Fashion week in their trench coats. With their neat prose and smart looks, these rapporteurs of the fashion world look 'just right' against the feverish atmosphere of the commercial style gala. So enraptured are they by the ceremonial donning of the trench, fashion insiders solemnly recite the adage that, 'Fashion Week wouldn't be complete without a classic trench coat sighting.'[1] When Susie Bubble, Oumayma Elboumeshouli and Alexa Chung (amongst many others) decide to wear trench coats to fashion events, they know exactly what they're doing. Trench coats have lineage.

In the last century the trench coat has been caught up in conflict, labour relations, policing, and gender politics. While it might be tempting to interpret the trench coat as a kind of war memorial, this does not fully explain its resonance in contemporary culture, nor does it account for such longevity. War birthed the design, but the trench coat underwent various transmutations as the excess of war spilled over into other conflicts, altering its meaning beyond all recognition. It attracted groups as various as patriots, feminists, journalists, artists, designers, philosophers, guerrillas, actors, and adorned characters in film, art, literature, and theatre. Resonating with those who recognized the trench coat as a mode of equivocation, it mobilized performances of making and remaking the self. As it got sucked into various political conflicts, the coat evolved into an experiment in melding utility and fashion, a peculiarly twentieth century technique for domesticating violence. A certain ambiguity made it a fulcrum for the realigning of loyalties. At opportune moments, adopting the mantle of the oppressor was found to have its own power for those marginalized by the prevailing social order.

Trench coats are tough and reliable; they've got you covered. They are trustworthy. Or so style briefings would have us believe. Few garments resist irrelevance in the fast-moving fashion cycle, but the trench coat remains sacrosanct. Perhaps the trench coat is more sacred than profane; in possession of shape-shifting powers, a cover for modesty, and a venerated accessory to mark transitions, it emerges as a talisman for modernity. It is as if the fashion industry—normally given to fickle and wasteful decisions—gives up its restless search to settle on a style, to finally admit, 'Well, that's it.' I am not suggesting that the trench coat reaches aesthetic perfection; far from it. Worn out, drab, banal, dissolute, stale, mundane, formless—trench coats are hardly objects of desire. Obscured by a prosaic exterior, their seductive qualities have nonetheless inspired glowing epithets, amongst them 'classic,' 'iconic,' 'a staple,' and 'effortless'. It is curious to witness a symbol of restraint, utility and tradition winning out against the stylistic battles, gatekeeping practices and sharp commercial decisions that constitute fashion business.

I can see why a techno-garment that defied the natural laws of porous fabrics and bodies might have attracted early adopters of the design. Fascination with the trench coat now, though, has much more to do with its imaginative potential, its multiple applications, its facility to camouflage, to blend, to provide cover. To protect the specialist entering a forbidding toxic environment, the coat holds all the properties of a protective suit of armour, yet the designation is purely symbolic. As a symbol of autonomous action and moral courage it has accompanied various figures—fictional and otherwise—on perilous journeys into unknown realms. More importantly, cultural narratives have given it a reputation for anointing those who journey to boundaries and edges. It promises sovereignty—with dark undertones of the colonial quest—materializing a certain style of entering and moving through hostile territory. Significantly, it implies violence that rarely shows on the surface. By melding the characteristics of the soldier, explorer, reporter, and settler, the trench coat authorizes access to new realms. Dangerous fantasies of power are mobilized by images of trench-coated figures.

If the trench coat lost its imperious attitude, then its dissolution joined our own, but it still proved to be imperishable; it transformed, mutated, and survived. Trench coats speak to primal regions of toil and sacrifice, reflecting the human impulse to venture out. It might be the sartorial uniform of style rapporteurs, but the trench coat cannot be fully understood through a fashion lens. It is so much more. If it prompts uncharacteristic claims to truth in a business predicated on illusion, then this suggests the trench coat's appeal to myth. Most of all, it allows you to feel 'just right'—of your time, socially placed, empowered, resolved, protected, contained. But what does the trench coat say about how we relate to our surroundings? Why are we so pleased with a designed object that enables us to recoil from an environment offering all manner of pleasures, possibilities, and creative encounters? In our stubborn insistence upon the individual sovereignty the trench coat affords, we betray a desire to be *disembedded*. Alongside a range of designs that we hold dear, the trench coat reflects a dubious humanism that stubbornly resists non-human forces and energies.

Coated by an impervious fabricated skin, the trench coat appeals to a sense of foreboding about our place in the world. It encases the human body, lending it a false sense of coherence. By comporting our bodies in such a defensive gesture, trench coats betray a fragile sense of self; their ubiquity reveals a struggle to accommodate a fearful, brittle core. Our attachment to the trench coat bespeaks a culture in retreat from itself, at war with its environment, shouldering a back catalogue of fears and anxieties too numerous to recall. It materializes and embodies a whole way of being intent on cutting off from the flow of influences, attachments, and entanglements waiting to be encountered 'out there'. Profoundly revealing of the defensiveness that conditioned the making of this sartorial archetype, the trench coat keeps us aloof from turbulent realities.

The coat stands in, too, for our relentless obsession with coverage, surfaces, skin. A membrane to encase (and embrace) bodies, it promises to make us whole by marking a safe and secure boundary between insides and outsides. The garment's sheer vitality might have catapulted it through the twentieth century and beyond, but this symbolic and material attempt to reconcile insides and outsides is riddled with contradiction. Deflective and ever on the move, the trench coat broke down binaries of military and civilian, admitting the insecurity of an environment built on violence. In this sense, the trench coat is inherently perverse. Bearing witness to the polluting influence of militarism on civil society, this coat captures the collective retreat from certainty throughout the last century, betraying too a sense of trepidation about the external world. It is, of course, no protection at all; but this imaginary shield against external threats might sum up the (post)modern malaise. Its failures remind us that we are not impervious. Neither can we design our way out of our present troubles. The trench coat might be a hollow consolation, but for now we remain compelled to succumb to its vital embrace.

POSTSCRIPT

The trench coat is a versatile all-purpose, practical piece of outerwear, the Swiss army knife of the wardrobe. Let's go over the external features of this iconic design one more time. While there are many varieties, the classic trench coat usually has the following features:

- Weatherproofed textile (essential)
- Shoulder epaulettes (originally to carry headwear)
- Double-breasted (for warmth)
- Belt with buckle (but not always)
- Sleeve loops (to keep the cold out)
- Two pockets (usually large, originally for military maps)
- Storm flap or 'gun flap' (to let water run away from the body, or to rest a gun)
- D-rings (military function only, to carry ammunition)
- Buttons (classic variety)
- Drab colour (again classic)

ACKNOWLEDGMENTS

would like to thank Christopher Schaberg and Ian Bogost for support and feedback on the manuscript. Thanks also to Haaris Naqvi and Rachel Moore for steering the project and nudging me along. I moved country soon after starting this project, but as it turned out, my arrival in a strange city during lockdown provided just enough alienation and isolation to settle into writing a book on the trench coat. I survived with the support of faculty colleagues at Vrije Universiteit Amsterdam, but I particularly want to thank Ivo Blom for sharing his valuable insights on trench coats in cinema. Thanks to friends willing to engage in idle chats on the topic and to my son, Dylan Tynan, who always offers a fresh perspective. And finally, special thanks must go to my partner Matt French for endless cups of tea, feedback on several drafts, and most of all for believing in me.

NOTES

Introduction

1 Bertrand M. Patenuade, "Mexico Centennials: Exile and Murder in Mexico," *Berkeley Review of Latin American Studies*, 2010. Author suggests that underneath the trench coat was a dagger, a handgun, and a pickaxe, not an ice pick as is commonly believed. The pickaxe was used to kill Trotsky in his study in August 1940.

Chapter 1

1 Virginia Woolf, *Mrs Dalloway*, (Oxford: Oxford University Press, 1998 [1925]), 14.

2 Jane Bennett, *Vibrant Matter: A Political Ecology of Things* (Durham: Duke University Press, 2010), 112.

3 Eduardo Viveiros de Castro, "Cosmological Deixis and Amerindian Perspectivism," *The Journal of the Royal Anthropological Institute*, 4, no. 3 (1988): 482.

4 Christopher N. Gamble, Joshua S. Hanan and Thomas Neil, "What is New Materialism?" *Angelaki,* 24, no. 6 (2019): 112.

5 Diana Coole and Samantha Frost, eds. *New Materialisms: Ontology, Agency and Politics* (Durham and London: Duke University Press, 2010).

6 Bruno Latour, *An Inquiry into Modes of Existence: An Anthropology of the Moderns* (Camb, Mass: Harvard University Press), 231.

7 Elizabeth Wilson, *Adorned in Dreams: Fashion in Modernity* (London: Vintage, 1985), 3.

8 Exhibition *Items: Is Fashion Modern?* Museum of Modern Art, New York. Oct 1 2017–Jan 28 2018. Catalogue Trench Coat Entry, "T-103." In *Items: Is Fashion Modern?* eds. Paola Antonelli and Michelle Millar Fisher, (New York: MoMA, 2017), 257–58.

9 John Tully, *The Devil's Milk: A Social History of Rubber* (New York: NYU Press, 2011), 36.

10 Sarah Levitt, "Manchester Mackintoshes: A History of the Rubberized Garment Trade in Manchester," *Textile History*, 17, no. 1 (1986): 51–69.

11 John Tully, *The Devil's Milk: A Social History of Rubber* (New York: NYU Press, 2011).

12 Ibid, 53.

13 Ibid, 41.

14 Levitt, "Manchester Mackintoshes," 55–56.

15 Ibid, 56.

16 Geraldine Biddle-Perry, "Fashionably Rational: the evolution of uniformed leisure in late nineteenth-century Britain" in

Uniform: Clothing and Discipline in the Modern World, eds. Jane Tynan and Lisa Godson (London: Bloomsbury, 2019), 109–34.

17 Max Weber, *The Protestant Work Ethic and the Spirit of Capitalism* (London and New York: Routledge, [1904] 2006).

18 "'Heptonette", Cloaks.' *Jordan Marsh & Co. Dept Store*, Dry Goods Catalog, Massachusetts, Boston, 18. Accessed 4 August 2021: https://archive.org/details/pricelist00jord/page/18/mode/1up?view=theater&q=wet

19 "Ladies and Misses' Mackintoshes."

20 "Genuine Macintosh Waterproofs," *Alamy*, M41X5H. c. 1900.

21 Celia Marshik, "The Modern(ist) Mackintosh," *Modernism/Modernity*, 19, no.1 (2012): 46.

22 David Trotter, *Literature in the First Media Age* (Camb, Mass: Harvard University Press, 2013), 112.

23 James Munson and Richard Mullen, *The Smell of the Continent: The British Discover Europe 1814–1914* (London: Pan MacMillan, 2010), 219.

Chapter 2

1 Gary J. Clifford and Robert P. Patterson *The World War I Memoirs of Robert P. Patterson: A Captain in the Great War* (Knoxville: University of Tennessee Press, 2012), 18.

2 Letter in *Financial Times* from Andrew McCarthy, 22 February 2019.

3 "Burberry Top-Coats," *The Sphere*, 24 Nov 1913, p. v. Mary Evans Picture Library, no: 10693671.

4   "The Burberry," *Punch*, 3 June 1914, p. ix. Burberry Archive, London.

5   Catherine Moriarty, "'Remnants of Patriotism': The Commemorative Representation of the Greatcoat after the First World War," *Oxford Art Journal*, 27, no. 3 (2004): 295.

6   Moriarty, "Remnants of Patriotism," 294.

7   Entry "coat." Accessed 5 August 2021: https://www.etymonline.com/word/coat. Also entry "coat." In *Chambers English Dictionary* (Edinburgh: Chambers Harrap Publishers, 2007), 231.

8   "Britain's 'Blue' and "Khaki" Boys," Advertisement, *The Tatler*. 1 Dec 1915, Mary Evans Picture Library, no: 10691345.

9   *Dress Regulations for the Army* (HMSO: Imperial War Museum, 1911), 11.

10 "Zambrene—Triple-Triple Proof" poster. 1914–1918. Imperial War Museum. ID: IWM ART. PST 13697.

11 "Aquascutum waterproof military coats," advertisement 1916. Mary Evans Picture Library. No: 11100035.

12 Paul Fussell, *The Great War and Modern Memory* (Oxford: Oxford University Press, 1975), 50.

13 Siegfried Sassoon, *Memoirs of a Fox-Hunting Man* (Norfolk: Faber, 1974 [1928]), 301–2.

14 Sassoon, *Memoirs of a Fox-Hunting Man*, 301–2.

15 Fussell, *The Great War and Modern Memory*, 74.

16 Mary Douglas, *Purity and Danger: An Analysis of the Concepts of Pollution and Taboo* (London: Routledge, 1966), 40.

Chapter 3

1 George Augustus Sala, *Dutch pictures: With Some Sketches in the Flemish Manner* (Vizetelly, 1883), 160.

2 George Orwell, *The English People* (London: Collins, 1947), 7.

3 Ibid, 8.

4 Alan S.G. Ross, "U and Non-U: An Essay in Sociological Linguistics." In *Noblesse Oblige: An Enquiry into the Identifiable Characteristics of the English Aristocracy,* ed. Nancy Mitford (London: Penguin, 1959 [1956]), 26.

5 Marshik, "The Modern(ist) Mackintosh," 46.

6 "Nine Women Reveal the Dangers of Working in a Munitions Factory," Imperial War Museum. Accessed 4 August 2021: https://www.iwm.org.uk/history/9-women-reveal-the-dangers-of-working-in-a-first-world-war-munitions-factory

7 Ibid.

8 "Female Factory Workers—World War One," 1916. *Getty Images.* No: 514490724.

9 "Great War Greenwich," *Memories of War.* Accessed 4 August 2021: http://www.memoriesofwar.org.uk/page/about_us?path=0p37p

10 "The First Aid Yeomanry on the Western Front *1914–1918.*" Petrol distribution to members of the First Aid Nursing Yeomanry (FANY), Unit 4, attached to the Belgian Army. Imperial War Museum Collection. ID: Q107954.

11 "Advertisement, Junior Stores," 15 Regent Street. n.d.

12 Ibid.

13 Juliette Pattinson, *Women of War: Gender, modernity and the First Aid Yeomanry* (Manchester: Manchester University Press, 2020), 101.

14 Cited in Linda J. Quiney, *The Small Army of Women: Canadian Volunteer Nurses and the First World War*, (Vancouver: UBC Press, 2017), 102.

15 "A woman from West Virginia who worked for the Red Cross Motor Corps photographed in Washington, D.C. 1917." Library of Congress. ID: hec.09023.

16 "Women of the Red Cross Motor Corps in WW1," National Women's History Museum, 19 October 2018. Accessed 13 May 2021: https://www.womenshistory.org/articles/women-red-cross-motor-corps-wwi

17 Sarah Glassford and Amy Shaw, *A Sisterhood of Suffering and Service: Women and Girls of Canada and Newfoundland during the First World War* (Vancouver: UBC Press, 2013), 132.

18 "VADs driver" Ernest Brooks. c. 1918. National Library of Scotland Collection. ID: CC BY 4.0

19 Pattison, *Women of War,* 102.

20 Elizabeth Cobbs, *The Hello Girls* (Camb, Mass: Harvard University Press, 2019), 61.

21 Ibid, 63.

22 Krisztina Roberts citing *Times*, August 17, 1914 and December 21, 1914, in "All That is best of the Modern Woman: Representations of Female Military Auxiliaries in British Popular Culture, 1914–1919" in *British Popular Culture and the First World War*, ed. Jessica Meyer (Leiden: Brill), 111.

23 "Barkers Women's Service Section," *The Tatler*, 19 December 1917. Mary Evans Picture Library. No: 10724351.

24 Ibid.

25 "Women's Trench Coats Sought," *The New York Times*, 31 July 1918.

26 Cheryl Buckley, "De-Humanized Females and Amazonians:' British Wartime Fashion and its Representation in Home Chat, 1914–1918," *Gender and History*, 14, no. 3 (2002): 532.

27 "Gifts for the Woman in Service, at Home and Abroad," *Harper's Bazaar*, November 1918, 66.

28 Helen Zenna Smith, *Not So Quiet…Stepdaughters of War* (London: George Newnes, 1930), 163.

29 Zenna Smith, *Not So Quiet…Stepdaughters of War*, 170–71.

30 Lucy Noakes "Playing at Being Soldiers:' British women and military uniform in the First World War," in *British Popular Culture and the First World War*, ed. Jessica Meyer (Leiden: Brill), 125.

Chapter 4

1 "Jean-Paul Sartre and Simon de Beauvoir in Paris." Porte d'Orleans in June 1929. Photo by JAZZ EDITIONS / Gamma-Rapho via Getty Images. ID: 117099183.

2 Jeff Shantz, *Against All Authority: Anarchism and the Literary Imagination* (Exeter: Imprint Academic, 2011), 50.

3 Marshik, "The Modern(ist) Mackintosh," 43.

4 James Joyce, *Ulysses* (New York: Random House, 1946 [1920]), 108, 251, 327, 475.

5 Paul Fussell, *The Great War and Modern Memory* (Oxford: Oxford University Press, 1975), 189.

6 Marshik, "The Modern(ist) Mackintosh," 44.

7 Nick Tabor, "No Slouch," *The Paris Review*, 7 April 2015.

8 W.B. Yeats, "The Second Coming," *W.B. Yeats: The Poems* ed. Daniel Albright (London: Random House), 235.

9 Gavin Foster, *The Irish Civil War and Society* (Basingstoke: Palgrave MacMillan, 2015), 95.

10 Tom Barry, *Guerilla Days in Ireland* (North Carolina: MacFarland, 2011 [1955]), 50.

11 Maurice Walsh, *Bitter Freedom: Ireland in a Revolutionary World 1918–1923* (London: Faber and Faber, 2015), 278.

12 T. Ryle Dwyer, *The Squad: And the Intelligence Operations of Michael Collins* (Cork: Mercier Press, 2005), 18.

13 Ernie O'Malley, *On Another Man's Wound,* (Dublin: Anvil Books [1936] 2002), 150.

14 Ibid, 219.

15 Elizabeth Bowen, *The Last September* (London: Vintage, 1998 [1929]), 33–34.

16 Cited in Peter Costello *The Heart Grown Brutal: The Irish Revolution in Literature, from Parnell to the death of Yeats 1891–1939* (Dublin: Gill and MacMillan, 1977), 159.

17 Ibid, 159.

18 Ibid, 177.

19 Photograph of IRA women scouts (n.d.) Plate 15. Costello *The Heart Grown Brutal.*

20 James Matthews *Voices: A Life of Frank O'Connor* (New York: Atheneum, 1983), 26.

21 Frank O'Connor, *The Best of Frank O'Connor* (New York: Random House, 2009), 91.

22 Ibid, 90.

23 R. F. Foster, *Modern Ireland 1600–1972* (London: Penguin), 500.

24 'Broad Black Brimmer' cited in Gavin Foster, *The Irish Civil War and Society* (Basingstoke: Palgrave MacMillan, 2015) 96. From *Irish Songs of Resistance*, Vol. 2, p. 1. N.D.

25 Foster, *The Irish Civil War and Society*, 96.

26 O'Malley, *On Another Man's Wound*, 252–58.

27 Aideen Carroll, *History Ireland* Vol. 6, Issue 5, 2008.

28 Éimear O'Connor, *Seán Keating: Art, Politics and Building the Irish Nation* (Newbridge: Irish Academic press, 2013), 132.

29 Ibid, 133.

30 Cited in Gregory A. Schirmer, *A History of Irish Poetry in English*, (Ithaca and London: Cornell University Press, 1998), 137. *Gombeen* is a term commonly used in Ireland (derived from modern Irish *gaimbín*) to describe a moneylender, usurer.

31 Photograph [Figure 27] in Dan Breen, *My Fight for Irish Freedom* (Cork: Mercier Press, 2010), facing page 145.

Chapter 5

1 Arnold Rampersad, *The Life of Langston Hughes: Vol 1: 1902–1941, I, Too, Sing America* (Oxford: Oxford University Press, 1986), 353.

2 Rampersad, *The Life of Langston Hughes*, 353.

3   Antonio Téllez Solà, *Sabaté: Urban Guerrilla in Spain* (Dais-Poynter Limited, 1974).

4   Marcella Hayes, "The Rebel Gesture: Anarchist Maquis of Barcelona 1939–60," in *Spanish Civil War and Its Memory*, eds. Molly Goodkind, Marcella Hayes and Amanda Mitchell, (Edicions Universitat Barcelona, 2015).

5   Marilyn Elkins, "The Fashion of Machismo," in *A Historical Guide to Ernest Hemingway*, ed. Linda Wagner-Martin, (Oxford: Oxford University Press, 2000), 98–99.

6   From The Complete Toronto "Star" Dispatches, 1920–1924, 10–11, cited in Elkins, "The Fashion of Machismo," 99.

7   Elkins, "The Fashion of Machismo," 104.

8   "Trenchcoats, Then and Now," *New York Times*, 24 June 1990.

9   Ibid.

10 Left to right: Roman Karmen, Ernest Hemingway and camera operator Ioris Iveno (Joris Ivens). Spain, 18 September 1937. SPUTNIK / *Alamy*.

11 Photograph from Nicholas Reynolds, *Writer, Sailor, Soldier, Spy: Ernest Hemingway's Secret Adventures, 1935–1961* (New York: William Morrow, 2017), 16. Original attribution: Fernhout Photo, Nederlands Fotomuseum.

12 Nicholas Reynolds, *Writer, Sailor, Soldier, Spy: Ernest Hemingway's Secret Adventures, 1935–1961* (New York: William Morrow, 2017), 15.

13 Linda Wagner-Martin, *Ernest Hemingway's A Farewell to Arms*, 40.

14 Lloyd R. Arnold, *Hemingway: High on the Wild* (New York: Grosset & Dunlop, 1977), 23.

15 Elkins, "The Fashion of Machismo,"103.

16 A.E. Hotchner, *Papa Hemingway: A Personal Memoir* (New York: Random House, 1966), 37.

17 Ibid, 128.

18 Ernest Hemingway *The Garden of Eden* (New York: Scribner, 1986), 38.

19 Howard R. Wolf, "Ernest Hemingway: After Such Knowledge…" *Cithara* 50, no. 2 (2011): 15. (last photo in the Lynn biography after page 337).

20 "Trenchcoats, Then and Now," *New York Times*, 24 June 1990.

21 Cited in Greg McLaughlin, *The War Correspondent* (London: Pluto, 2002), 19.

22 Kate Darnton, Kayce Freed Jennings, Lynn Sheer, eds. *Peter Jennings: A Reporter's Life*, (New York: Public Affairs, 2007), 41–42.

Chapter 6

1 Sheri Chinen Biesen, "Censoring and Selling Film Noir," *Censura e auto-censura*, A Bibbó, S. Ercolino, M. Lino (eds) *Between,* V 9 (2015): 1.

2 Uğur Ümit Üngör, *Paramilitarism: Mass Violence in the Shadow of the State* (Oxford: Oxford University Press, 2020), 30.

3 Ibid, 62.

4 Ibid, 30.

5 Stella Bruzzi, *Undressing Cinema: Clothing and Identity in the Movies* (London: Routledge, 1997), 70.

6 Sheri Chinen Biesen, "Censoring and Selling Film Noir,"
Between, vol V, n 9 (2015), 2.

7 Ula Lukszo "Noir Fashion and Noir as Fashion," in *Fashion in
Film*, ed. Adrienne Munich (Bloomington and Indianapolis:
Indiana University Press, 2011), 75–76.

8 Sheri Chinen Biesen, "Classic Hollywood and American Film
Censorship," *The American Historian*. Accessed 23 July 2021:
https://www.oah.org/tah/issues/2019/history-and-the-movies
/classic-hollywood-and-american-film-censorship/>

9 Joel Dinerstein, *The Origins of Cool in Postwar America*
(Chicago: Chicago University Press, 2017), 74.

10 Jack Nachbar, "Doing the Thinking for All of Us: *Casablanca*
and the Home Front," *Journal of Popular Film and Television*,
27, no. 4 (2000): 5–15.

11 Raymond Chandler, *The Big Sleep* (London: Penguin, 1970
[1939]), 32.

12 Chandler, *The Big Sleep*, 39–41.

13 Stanley Orr, *Darkly Perfect World: Colonial Adventure,
Postmodernism and American Film Noir* (Columbus: Ohio
State University Press, 2010).

14 Ibid, 74.

15 Ibid, 72.

16 Marilyn Cohen, "Out of the Trenches and into Vogue: Un-
Belting the Trench Coat" in *Fashion Crimes: Dressing for
Deviance*, ed. Joanne Turney (London: Bloomsbury, 2019)
157–167.

17 Megan E. Abbott, "'Nothing You Can't Fix:' Screening
Marlowe's Masculinity," *Studies in the Novel*, 35, no. 3 (2003):
307.

18 Chandler, *The Big Sleep*, 172–73.

19 Edward Dimendberg, *Film Noir and the Spaces of Modernity* (Camb, Mass: Harvard University Press, 2004), 171.

20 Chandler, *The Big Sleep*, 222.

Chapter 7

1 Lukszo "Noir Fashion and Noir as Fashion," 56.

2 Christopher Sharrett, "Jack Webb and the Vagaries of Right-Wing TV Entertainment," *Cinema Journal*, 51, no. 4 (2012): 166.

3 Luc Boltanksi, *Mysteries and Conspiracies* (Cambridge: Polity, 2014), 30.

4 Robert van Hallberg, *The Maltese Falcon to Body of Lies: Spies, Noir and Trust* (Albuquerque: University of New Mexico Press, 2015), 14–15.

5 Sharrett, "Jack Webb and the Vagaries of Right-Wing TV Entertainment," 167.

6 Joseph W. Slade, "Romanticizing Cybernetics in Ridley Scott's Blade Runner," *Film Quarterly*, 18, no. 1 (1990): 14.

7 Ibid, 14.

8 Joel Dinerstein, *The Origins of Cool in Postwar America,* (Chicago: Chicago University Press, 2017), 121.

9 Ibid, 122–24.

10 Ibid, 131.

11 "Pablo Picasso, 1933." Photograph by Man Ray, THE MET. Accessed 7 August 2021: https://www.metmuseum.org/art/collection/search/265221

12 Michael Moorcock, *London Peculiar and Other Nonfiction* (CA: PM Press, 2012), 20.

13 Ibid, 130.

14 Nancy Hass, "The People James Baldwin Knew," *The New York Times*, 11 December 2020.

15 Ibid.

16 James Miller, *The Passion of Michel Foucault* (London: HarperCollins, 1993), 148.

17 Ibid, 149.

Chapter 8

1 Stella Bruzzi, *Undressing Cinema: clothing and identity in the movies* (London: Routledge, 1997), 99.

2 Jake Gallagher, "One Icon, One Detail: Gordon Parks' Trench Coat," *Esquire*, 29 May 2013.

3 Guy Trebay, "Gordon Parks was the Godfather of Cool," *The New York Times*, 4 February 2021.

4 Judy Klemesrud, "Shaft—'A Black Man Who is for Once a Winner,'" *The New York Times*, 12 March 1972.

5 Antonia Finnane, *Changing Clothes in China: Fashion, History, Nation* (New York: Colombia University Press, 2008), 258.

6 Ibid, 258.

7 "Weather Report: Return of the Trench," *Vogue* (US), vol. 120, issue 2, 1952, 90–91.

8 Kate Finnigan, "The best trench coats for men and women," *Financial Times*, 8 February 2019.

9 Ornella K. Pistilli "The Heritage-Creativity Interplay: How Fashion Designers are Reinventing Heritage as Modern Design," *ZoneModa Journal*, 8, no. 1 (2018): 93.

10 Ulrich Lehmann, *Tigersprung: Fashion in Modernity* (Camb, Mass: MIT Press, 2000).

11 Elizabeth Wilson, *Adorned in Dreams: Fashion in Modernity* (London: Vintage, 1985).

12 Ibid, 15.

13 "Trench Coats—How to wear," *Sunday Times* (UK) 24 March 2018, 6.

14 Florence Kane, "Digging the Trench," *Vogue* (US) vol. 196, issue 12, 2006, 214.

15 Bill Doll, "Trench Coat Man," *Fortune Small Business*, 10, 7, 2000, 124.

16 June Weir, "The Trench-Coat Mystique," *The New York Times*, 4 March 1984, 697.

17 "Turn Coats," *Vogue* (US) Vol. 194, issue 4, 1 April 2004, 210.

18 "Closet Classic: Every Woman Needs a Trench Coat," *Redbook*, vol. 220, issue 4, April 2013, 104.

19 Ibid, 104.

20 Na'ama Klorman-Eraqi, "Underneath we're Angry: Feminism and Media Politics in Britain in the late 1970s and early 1980s," *Feminist Media Studies*, 17, no. 2 (2017): 231–47.

21 Ibid, 231.

22 Lyall Bush "Consuming Hemingway: 'The Snows of Kilimanjaro' in the Postmodern Classroom" *The Journal of Narrative Technique,* 25, no. 1 (1995): 29.

23 Samantha Conti, "Burberry Expands Social Networking," *WWD: Women's Wear Daily*, vol. 198, issue 98, 2009.

24 Ibid.

25 Khaoula Ghanem, "But First, Let Me Take a Selfie: Burberry's Art of the Trench Campaign Looks to the Middle East to Bolster Profits," *Vogue*, 13 April 2016. Accessed 4 August 2021: https://en.vogue.me/archive/legacy/burberry-art-of-the -trench-campaign-event-dubai/

Conclusion

1 "Showgoers wore their best trench coats on day 5 of London Fashion week," *Fashionista*, 20 September 2017. Accessed 5 August 2021: At: https://fashionista.com/2017/09/london -fashion-week-spring-2018-street-style-day-5

INDEX

A Foreign Affair
        (Wilder)   103–5
advertisements   3–4, 19–20,
        26, 32, 36, 40, 73,
        128–9, 131
AEF *see* American
        Expeditionary Forces
Afro-futurism   135
alienation   77, 81, 84, 115
Alphaville (Godard)   108–9
American Expeditionary
        Forces (AEF)   21
American Red Cross   42, 79
anarchism   54–5, 57, 59–60, 67
Angry Young Men   114
anonymity   4, 38, 55–6, 59
anti-colonialism   57, 65–6
Aquascutum   22–3, 26–7
assassin   108

Baldwin, James   115
banality   1, 51, 138
Barry, Tom   59
Bennett, Jane   8

Berlin, Germany   103
Beyoncé   2, 135–6
Bladerunner (Scott)   109–11
Bladerunner 2049
        (Villeneuve)   111–12
Bogart, Humphrey   90, 92,
        100–101, 113, 126
boundaries   4, 58, 67, 70, 88–
        9, 97, 107, 139, 141 (*see
        also* gender boundaries
        and fluidity)
Boltanski, Luc   107
Bowen, Elizabeth   61
Breen, Dan   68
Bubble, Susie   137
Burberry   22, 27, 35–7, 81,
        130–1

camouflage   27–8, 58, 62,
        127, 132, 139
Camus, Albert   113
capitalism   12, 17, 35, 68,
        109, 125
Casablanca (Curtiz)   90–1, 126

Chandler, Raymond   86, 95–9, 107
Chinese Cultural Revolution   122
Cho, Aimee   126
Cold War, the   104–5, 107
Collins, Michael   59–60
colonialism   15, 20, 56, 70, 97, 104, 126, 139 (*see also* anti-colonialism)
Costello, Peter   63
Coward, Rosalind   129
Cronkite, Walter   82
cultural narratives   3, 125, 129, 139
cultural objects   1, 125

de Beauvoir, Simone   1–2, 54, 114
Delaney, Beauford   115
detective fiction   86–101, 107–8
detectives   59, 87, 95, 99, 104–7, 119
disembeddedness   130, 140
Douglas, Mary   30–1
Dragnet (Webb)   104–6
dystopia   31, 108, 111–12, 132

Elkins, Marilyn   73, 79
Enfield, Lee (rifle)   63
environmental degradation   12, 14, 110–11

epaulettes   26–7, 42, 47, 83, 143
Existentialism   113, 116

fabric   2, 8, 12, 14, 16, 22, 30, 139
fabulations   4, 132
factories   14–16, 20, 27–8, 37–8
Fallon, Gabriel   61
fantasies   6, 26–7, 29–32, 39, 82, 96, 104, 115, 135, 139
FANY *see* First Aid Nursing Yeomanry, militarized femininity
Fashion Week   138
femininity   39, 75, 103, 122, 127 (*see also* militarized femininity)
feminism   43, 127 (*see also* femininity, gender boundaries and fluidity)
film noir   86–9
First World War
    industrialized battlefield   28
    movies   112
    societal militarization   65, 67
    trench coat   1, 13, 22, 33, 48, 56, 65, 124
    United Kingdom   24, 38

Western Front 21–2, 29, 31, 40, 43
women workers 38–51
writing 30
post–war period 54, 56–8
see also Hemingway, Ernest; *Memoirs of a Fox-Hunting Man*
Foreign Correspondent (Hitchcock) 69–70
Foster, Gavin 64–5
Foucault, Michel 116–17
Fussell, Paul 28, 30, 55–6

Gamages 25
Gaultier, Jean Paul 127
gender boundaries and fluidity 43–4, 48, 50
Gosling, Armine 43
Great Depression, the 86, 95, 97
gun flap 63, 143
Gvasalia, Demna 132

Harper's Bazar 48
Harriman, Florence J. Borden 42
Hays Production Code 89, 93
Hemingway, Ernest 2, 73–83
    Garden of Eden 81
    For Whom the Bell Tolls 75
    Sun Also Rises, The 77

heritage 36, 125–6, 130
Hughes, Langston 70, 72

Imperial War Museum 1, 26, 40
industrialization 10, 14–17, 33, 130
    on the battlefield 28, 39, 49
International Brigades 70–1, 77
Irish War of Independence 57–68
    Dáil Éireann 57–8
    Irish Citizen Army 58
    Irish Republican Army (IRA) 58–60, 62–66
    Sinn Féin 57
    see also Juno and the Paycock; Men of the South; O'Malley, Ernie
Ivens, Joris 77

Joyce, James 55–6
Juno and the Paycock (O'Casey) 61

Karmen, Roman 75–6
Keating, Seán 65–6
Kenneth Durward 26
Kinsella, Thomas 67
Kiss Me Deadly (Aldrich) 93, 128

Latour, Bruno   10
Laura (Preminger)   87–8
leisure and recreation   2,
         17–19, 22, 36, 46–8, 50
leisure clothes   17–18, 36,
         46–7
lifestyles   17–18, 36–7
London Fog   126
London *Times,* the   46
longevity (of trench coat)   9,
         126, 137
Lukszo, Ula   89

Macintosh, Charles   14–15
Margiela, Martin   126
Marlowe, Philip   2, 95–100,
         104
Marshik, Celia   56
masculinity   25, 44–5, 75–8, 81,
         83–4, 90, 96, 98, 100–1,
         104–5, 114, 128
mass–production   15, 19,
         28–9, 33, 37, 122
material   1, 8–13, 15, 17–18,
         29–30, 32, 55, 74, 80, 141
Matrix, The
         (Wachowskis)   132–135
McQueen, Alexander   126
mechanization   16
*Memoirs of a Fox-Hunting
         Man* (Sassoon)   30–1
Men of the South
         (Keating)   65–6

militarized femininity   39–51
    First Aid Nursing
         Yeomanry (FANY)
         40–1
    Voluntary Aid Detachment
         (VADs)   40–1, 43, 48
    see also American
         Red Cross; gender
         boundaries and fluidity
Miller, Henry   114
Mitford, Nancy   36–7
modernity   2–3, 10–11, 16,
         28–31, 48–50, 55–7,
         80, 84, 115, 125, 138
         (*see also* femininity;
         industrialization;
         militarized femininity)
morality   17, 25, 82, 89,
         91–3, 97, 104, 109–10,
         113, 139
Mrs Dalloway (Woolf)   7
Museum of Modern Art (New
         York City)   11

New Materialisms   9–10
New York Times, the   47, 127
Noakes, Lucy   50
Noblesse Oblige (Mitford)   36,
normalization (of
         violence)   30, 32–3

O'Casey, Seán   61, 63
O'Connor, Éimear   66

O'Connor, Frank   63–4
officers (military)   22–6, 28, 65, 73
O'Malley, Ernie   60, 65
Owens, Rick   132
Orwell, George   35–6
    The English People   35

paramilitarism   87–8
paranoia   89, 104–5, 107, 120
Paris, France   54, 78, 80, 115
Parks, Gordon   119, 121
Pattinson, Juliette   45
patriotism   25, 45–7, 53, 137
Picasso, Pablo   114
Pistilli, Ornella   125
police   59, 87, 99, 119, 135
Port of Shadows (Carné)   85–6
post–war society   77, 84, 91, 97, 104–5, 109, 115
Prohibition   86
Protestant work ethic   17
Pugh, Gareth   132

raincoats   15–18, 22, 26, 29, 36, 71, 126
reinvention   2, 124–6, 135
reporters (correspondents)   69–70, 75–6, 82–3, 126, 139
revolution   57, 60, 64, 67, 70, 116, 122 (*see also* Irish War of Independence)
Ross, Alan S. C.   36

rubber   13–16
    rubber barons   15

Sabaté, Quico   71–2
Saint Laurent, Yves   95, 127
Sala, George Augustus   36
Sartre, Jean–Paul   54, 116
science-fiction   109–11, 114
Second World War   51, 69, 71, 75, 81–2, 86, 90–1, 104, 124
seduction   19, 96, 98, 138
shadowy trench coated figure   53–5, 60–1, 85–95, 111
Shaft (Parks)   119–121
Shantz, Jeff   54
silhouettes   25, 47, 91
social class   35–6, 45, 56
Solo: A Star Wars Story (Howard)   112
Spanish Civil War   70–2, 75–6
Spanish Maquis   71
storm flap   40, 63, 143
Strauss, Claude Lévi   20
"Subterranean Homesick Blues" (Dylan)   4
subversiveness   68, 89, 105–8, 121
suffering   14–15, 31–2, 55
suffragism   39, 42–3, 45, 49, 56

tailoring   16, 24–5, 27, 29, 73
Tatler, The   25, 47
textiles   2, 111, 143
The Big Sleep (Chandler)   95
The Big Sleep (Hughes)
      95–101 (*see also*
      Marlowe, Philip)
The Last September
      (Bowen)   61
The Man Who Was Thursday
      (Chesterton)   54
The Third Man (Reed)   91,
      109
Thresher   21–2
trenchcoat prose   70, 72
Trotsky, Leon   4
Trotter, David   20

Ulysses (Joyce)   55
Üngör, Uğur Ümit   88
uniform   1, 24–5, 27–9, 31–2,
      37–51, 59–60, 63, 66–8,
      71–4, 76, 108, 124, 127,
      135–6, 140

Vogue Magazine   113, 124,
      127
VADs *see* Voluntary
      Aid Detachment,
      militarized femininity
vulcanization   15–16, 18

weapons   4, 58, 62–3, 71–2,
      135
Weber, Max   17
women's liberation   51
Woolf, Virginia   7, 9, 56
workers   15–16, 19,
      37–9, 47

Yeats, William Butler   57–8,
      63

Zambrene   26